THE CHALLENGE OF CENTRAL ASIA

*A Brief Survey of Tibet and its Borderlands, Mongolia,
North-West Kansu, Chinese Turkistan, and
Russian Central Asia.*

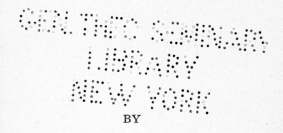

BY

MILDRED CABLE . F. HOUGHTON . R. KILGOUR .
A. McLEISH . R. W. STURT . AND OLIVE WYON.

WORLD DOMINION PRESS,

1, TUDOR STREET, LONDON, E.C. 4
113, FULTON STREET, NEW YORK CITY
632–634, CONFEDERATION LIFE BUILDING, TORONTO, CANADA

1929

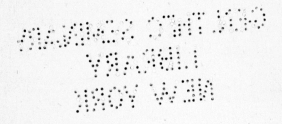
PRINTED BY
WILSON'S PRINTING COMPANY, LTD.,
67b, TURNMILL STREET,
LONDON, E.C. I.

Printed in Great Britain.

PREFACE

THE aim of this series is to describe briefly and clearly the situation in the various countries of the world as viewed from the standpoint of the Kingdom of God.

An earlier Survey of Central Asia, now out of print, revealed the need for a much more complete account of the religious situation in this area. This Survey is a complete restatement.

The nucleus of this book is the work of Miss Mildred Cable, of the China Inland Mission. Other sections have been prepared by the Rev. Frank Houghton, of the China Inland Mission, the Rev. R. Kilgour, D.D., Editorial Superintendent of the British and Foreign Bible Society, Mr. R. W. Sturt, of the Brethren Mission, Miss Olive Wyon, of the World Dominion Press, and the Survey Editor of the World Dominion Movement.

Thanks are specially due to the secretaries of the various missionary societies for the help which they have given.

The maps have been prepared by Dr. Henry Fowler and Mr. R. W. Sturt.

The map of Central Asia will repay careful study. It should be noted that Russian Central Asia is now a greatly enlarged territory, containing nearly one-third of the population of the whole of Central Asia.

The term Central Asia is now defined as that region lying to the north of the main range of the Himalayas, thereby excluding Bhutan, Nepal, Kashmir and Afghanistan. The lands described have an area of 4,203,681 square miles, and a population of 34,155,954.

It will also be seen from the map how completely the whole region is dominated by the railway system of Soviet Russia, southern extensions of which have already been carried out, and more are contemplated.

From this it can readily be gathered how serious is the Soviet menace. The British policy of keeping these frontier lands as buffer states seems to have thrown them into the power of their northern neighbours. In the long run the three great powers, Russia, China and British India, will be involved in the task of deciding the future of Central Asia, and the whole region will then be opened to missionary effort. It behoves the Christian Church thoroughly to acquaint itself with the present situation, and by its prayers and efforts to help bring in the light of the Gospel, which alone can dispel the darkness and gladden the hearts of the peoples of these immense mountain tracts and extensive deserts and tablelands.

ALEXANDER MCLEISH,
Survey Editor.

1, TUDOR STREET, E.C. 4.
1st *October*, 1929.

CONTENTS

PAGE

PREFACE iii

Introduction.

I. CENTRAL ASIA IN WORLD HISTORY 9
II. EARLY AND MEDIEVAL MISSIONS IN CENTRAL ASIA 17

Chapter.

THE SITUATION IN CENTRAL ASIA TO-DAY.

I. RUSSIAN CENTRAL ASIA 31
II. CHINESE TURKISTAN (SINKIANG) 42
III. NORTH-WEST KANSU 53
IV. MONGOLIA 59
V. TIBET 77
VI. ON THE BORDERLAND OF TIBET 88
VII. THE CHALLENGE 104

Appendices.

INTRODUCTION : SUGGESTED POLICY OF MISSIONARY ADVANCE 111
STATISTICAL SUMMARY 114
I. RUSSIAN CENTRAL ASIA 114
II. CHINESE TURKISTAN (SINKIANG) 115
III. NORTH-WEST KANSU AND KANSU-TIBETAN BORDER .. 115
IV. MONGOLIA 116
V. TIBET 117
VI. CHINESE AND INDIAN BORDERLANDS 118
BIBLIOGRAPHY 119
CHRONOLOGICAL TABLES 122

Maps.

I. CENTRAL ASIA, SHOWING MISSION STATIONS .. Facing Preface
II. MONGOLIA, ILLUSTRATING CHINESE INFILTRATION Facing page 59
INDEX 129

Introduction

The Challenge of Central Asia

INTRODUCTION

I.

Central Asia in World History

(i.)

THREE great names dominate the story of Central Asia : Alexander the Great, Genghiz Khan and Timur. Of Alexander the Great* it has been said that he was " singular among men of action for the imaginative splendours which guided him, and among romantic dreamers for the things which he achieved."

It was in the year 334 B.C. that he turned his back upon Europe and began the great adventure of the conquest of the East. He overran Persia and penetrated into Afghanistan, struck north through the Hindu Kush into Turkistan and pressed forward to Samarkand and Bukhara. Against tremendous odds, and with cruel sufferings which the King shared with his soldiers, he finally led his war-weary veterans over the North-West Frontier into India, whence he returned through Baluchistan to Persia. Early in 323 Alexander went to Babylon, and there he died on the 13th of June, at the age of thirty-two. Young as he was when he died, Alexander had yet inaugurated a new epoch. " He is one of the few to whom it has been given to modify the whole future of the human race."†

As a true Greek, Alexander regarded the establishment of cities as essential to the spread of civilization, and, wherever he passed, towns and fortresses came

---

* 356–323 B.C.

† *Encyclopædia Britannica*, Vol. XII, p. 454. *Cf* also *Cambridge Ancient History*, Vol. VI, p. 436.

into being, many of which were called by his own name. Where Khojend now stands he founded the great fortress of " Farthest Alexandria " (*Alexandria Eschatê*). This was the final outpost of Hellenism, looking out over the Scythian Steppes and controlling the Central Asian trade route through Kashgar into China, whence came the riches of the East to the markets of Europe. A century later Demetrius realized that conquest of the East could only be maintained by the control of these trade routes, and for that purpose he extended his rule right up to the Pamirs.

Meanwhile rival nations, the Hsiung Nu and the Yueh Chi, were struggling for the supremacy in North China and Central Asia. The former held the land from the north of Shansi Province to Lake Barkul, and the latter settled in the territory forming the present Province of Kansu. The Chinese took vigorous measures to overcome the Hsiung Nu, and by 59 B.C. China had established her authority over the region which is now called Chinese Turkistan. A few years later fifty-five states of Western Tartary had declared themselves vassals of the Chinese Emperor.

Later on the Yueh Chi split into two branches, one of which mingled with the Tibetans, while the other became a very powerful tribe which held Kashgar for some time ; it finally disappeared before the White Huns in the fifth century.

A branch of the Yueh Chi known as the Kushans was responsible for the spread of Greek influence through Khotan, Yarkand and Kashgar into the heart of Central Asia. In recent years, traces of Greek and Babylonian influences have been found by Sir Aurel Stein at Khotan and at Tunghwang ; by Dr. Albert von Le Coq at Turfan and elsewhere ; and by the Swedish archaeologist, Dr. Anderson, in Kansu.

Chinese supremacy in Asia increased until the first century of the Christian era, when the Tibetans revolted, and for a time the Western countries were again cut off from China. The Great Wall, which had been in process of construction for three hundred years, was extended at this time as far as Tunghwang, where a military camp was established to guard the fortress against the Tibetans.

After a period of silence we find that the Tibetan people, who entered on their historical period towards the end of the sixth century, gained successive victories over the Chinese until the seventh century, when they became masters of the four garrisons that formed the Protectorate of Anhsi, a city which still commands the entrance to the Gobi Desert, and from whose walls the traveller still looks out on the arid waste. A quarter of a century later the Tibetans were in possession of Kashgaria, thus blocking the road of the Chinese to the west.

In A.D. 692 the Chinese retook the four garrisons of Central Asia which they had lost to Tibet : Karashar, Kuche, Kashgar and Khotan, and, owing to warfare between Tibet and other tribes, the Chinese frontier enjoyed a period of comparative peace.

Finally, in the eighth century, Tibetan power had to yield to the Uigurs, who became masters of the whole country from the Altai Range to Aksu. These Uigurs were a powerful people of Turkish race, descended from the Hsiung Nu. Their influence increased rapidly from the beginning of the eighth century, till it extended from Kashgar in the West to Honan, Central China, in the East.

It was in this Province that the Uigur commander met some priests of the Manichean religion, and was converted by them ; when he returned to the north he took with him four of these priests. This religion of Mani arose in Babylonia about the middle of the third century A.D., and during many generations it exercised a great influence both in the East and in the West. It claimed to be both a religion and a philosophy, since it set up a code of ethics and also supplied an explanation of the constitution of the world, in which it taught that humanity is of Satanic origin ; it was, however, scarcely a philosophy in the European sense of the word. By its teaching idolatry was strictly prohibited. It prevailed in Persia until the latter half of the eighth century, and it is believed that it was finally swept away by the great Mongol invasion of the thirteenth century.

In the ninth century the Uigurs suffered some defeats at the hands of the Kirghiz, and were scattered to the south and south-west towards Turfan and Hami, where their agricultural ability did much for the development of these amazingly fertile oases. Remnants of the Uigur people settled in Kansu in the border towns of Kanchow and Suchow, where clear traces of their descendants are still to be found.

(ii.)

With the rise of Genghiz Khan* Central Asia was drawn once more into the stream of world history. The forward march of the conquering Mongol hosts compelled Europe to recognize the tremendous forces concentrated in Central Asia.†

Emerging from the obscurity of their pastoral homes in the regions lying to the east and south of Lake Baikal, the Mongols first appeared about A.D. 1135 as one of the wild marauding Tartar tribes which had harassed China for centuries. Under the able leadership of Genghiz Khan, the " Scourge of God," the fierce mounted warriors swept down in resistless waves of conquest, east, west and south from the great grassy plains of the north, where at Karakorum the great Khan had established his world metropolis of tents and movable huts.‡

Thundering across the uplands of Central Asia, the wild and hardy horsemen carried terror and desolation far and wide. It was well for the city that opened its gates to receive them without resistance,

---

* 1162–1227 A.D. The most reliable account of Genghiz Khan in English is contained in Bartol'd's *Turkestan down to the Mongol Invasion.*

† This Mongolian invasion of Asia and Europe is the fourth of the *Nomadic Movements in Asia,* described by Sir E. Denison Ross in his *Aldred Lectures* on *The Arabs, the Turks, the Seljuks,* and *the Mongols.* —*Journal of the Royal Society of Arts,* 20th and 27th September ;   4th and 11th October, 1929.

‡ *I.e., Karakorum* in Mongolia.

else smoking ruins and piles of skulls and bleaching bones alone were left to tell the tale of those who refused to yield. During twelve years (1211–1223) over eighteen million people perished in North China and South Mongolia alone.

Genghiz Khan had mastered half the known world, and his name inspired a fear which lasted for generations.* Unlike the Empire of Alexander, the Mongol dominion did not fall to pieces with the death of its creator. The Mongol clans had been unified, and when, in 1227, Genghiz Khan died in Mongolia, he left to his sons an Empire which stretched from the China Sea to the banks of the Dnieper.

Genghiz Khan was more than "a cruel barbarian at the head of countless savage horsemen." Sir Denison Ross emphasizes the fact that although he and his successors " carried destruction and desolation into the fairest lands of Asia on an unprecedented scale, what he achieved in unifying his empire, in organizing his administration, and in codifying his laws, entitle him to unstinted admiration. As a world conqueror he does not yield in eminence even to Alexander the Great ; as a legislator he may fitly be compared to Napoleon ; as an administrator he showed a wonderful broadmindedness in choosing the right men to serve him no matter what their nationality ; as a general he was never out-manœuvred, and as a soldier he was the bravest of the brave."†

---

* His name " is commonly associated with the terrible invasions of Persia and Eastern Europe which were carried out by the forces which he had set in motion in the thirteenth century. It was in reality his grandson Hulagu who turned Bagdad into a smouldering charnel house, and it was another grandson, Batu, who invaded Europe. Chinghiz Khan himself never journeyed further west than the Oxus, or further south than the Indus. During his active career, extending over fifty years, he was fully occupied with the unification of the Tatar tribes, the conquest of Northern China, and the overthrow of the powerful king of the Eastern Provinces of the Islamic world. It was another grandson, the famous Kublai Khan, who completed the conquest of China, and founded the dynasty of the Yuan, which endured for seventy-five years (1257–1332)."—Sir E. Denison Ross in *Journal of the Royal Society of Arts*, 11th October, 1929, p. 1101.

† *Journal of the Royal Society of Arts*, 11th October, 1929, p. 1101.

The effect of this great conqueror upon the world was amazing. It is difficult to imagine what would have happened if he had not lived. So devastating was the storm of the Mongol conquests that wherever their armies had swept past men had to make a new beginning. In many lands civilization sprang up afresh. The growing power of Islam was broken ; Arabic ceased to be the universal language of scholars throughout one-half of the world. The Turks were driven westwards, and the Ottoman Turks finally captured Constantinople. Genghiz Khan had opened up the way between the East and the West ; the barriers of the Dark Ages were thrown down, and Europe came into contact with China.

For the moment, however, the contact was one of sheer terror and dismay. Genghiz Khan was succeeded by his son, Ogdai, who set himself to follow up his father's conquests. His armies went forth to the East and to the West, carrying all before them. In 1236 they invaded Georgia and Great Armenia, where they committed dreadful atrocities. They pushed on into Russia, burning and torturing as they went. " No eye remained open to weep for the dead." Moscow fell before their irresistible advance ; then Kiev was captured, its inhabitants massacred, and the city razed to the ground.

Dividing into two sections the Mongols poured into Poland and Hungary, and on Christmas Day, 1241, the Mongol general crossed the Danube on the ice and took Esztergom by assault. Panic-stricken Europe believed itself to be on the point of complete subjugation by the barbarian hordes.

Suddenly, by an act of God, the tide was stemmed, and the enormous army hastily withdrew eastwards in response to a peremptory command from head-quarters. The great leader Ogdai lay dead in distant Mongolia, and the campaign was abandoned. As the army withdrew, it carried away with it many European women, whose descendants are to be found among the Tartar tribes of the present day.

The Mongols soon became complete masters of

China and placed their Emperor, Kublai Khan, on the throne at Cambaluc (Khanbalag), the modern Peking. The splendour and enlightenment of his court became the wonder of Europe, and it was to this court that the Venetian travellers, the brothers Nicolo and Maffeo Polo made their way. The Khan was delighted with his European guests, and listened eagerly to their accounts of the Latin world. Finally, he sent them back to the Pope with letters from himself asking for a large body of educated men to teach Christianity to his people. It has been suggested that Kublai's main purpose was political, and that he desired Christian teaching in order to tame and subdue his wild subjects. When, however, Rome failed to respond to his request, he fell back upon Buddhism as his instrument of civilization.

The vast extent of the Tartar flood had obliterated all artificiality of racial prejudice from the Yellow River to the Danube, and the accidents of war and the opportunities of commerce inevitably carried a variety of persons, representing various classes of European life, into Central Asia. With the opening up of the trade routes Europe became curious to know more about " the East." Two centuries later Vasco da Gama set out on his journey by sea to the Indies, and when in August, 1492, Columbus set sail from Palos in Andalusia, the goal of his hopes was not America but " the land of the Great Khan."

(iii.)

Little more than a century elapsed before Central Asia was again the scene of another vast attempt to dominate the known world. Timur-i-Leng,* generally known as Tamerlane, was born in 1336 at Kesh, " the Green City," some fifty miles south of Samarkand. With fewer advantages than either Alexander or Genghiz Khan, Tamerlane achieved all that Alexander had been able to do. He gathered a people round him, conquered the military forces of more than half the

---

* "The lame Timur."   1336–1405 A.D.

world, levelled cities to the ground and rebuilt them
according to his fancy, and collected and spent the
treasures of empires.

As with Genghiz Khan, the westward march of
Timur affected the political situation and changed
the course of European history. Once more he opened
up the trade routes. The upheaval caused by his death
was a blow to trade with Asia, and this was one of the
reasons which impelled Columbus and Vasco da Gama
to try to discover the sea route to the Far East. In
Russia the Golden Horde* was crushed, and the
Russians were set free for their own national
development. In Central Asia itself Timur's death
caused the final separation between the warriors of
Turan in the north and the cultured peoples of Iran
in the south. To-day the descendants of the Mongols
and the Tartars—the Kirghiz and Kalmuk Tartars—
" graze their sheep and horses by the ruins of the
towers that Timur built."

(iv.)

Tamerlane was the last of the great conquerors,
but significant things are happening in Central Asia
in our own day. Throughout this whole region the
growing influence of Soviet Russia is the main factor
in contemporary politics. Some would even go so far
as to say that the return of Russia to Asia is one of
the most momentous changes which has taken place
in the world since 1914.

The " Eurasian " theory of Russia's political destiny
is being applied to the problems of Central Asia with a
large measure of success.

" Let us turn our faces towards Asia. The East
will help us to conquer the West." These words of
Lenin have been accepted by his followers. One of the
most important centres of Communist propaganda

---

* The name of a body of Tartars who overran a great part of
Eastern Europe in the middle of the thirteenth century. In Russia
they founded the Tartar empire, known as the Empire of the Golden
Horde or the western Kipchaks.

has been situated in Tashkent since March, 1928. A paper has been published in this city which bears the title *The Bulletin of the Middle Eastern Press*. Upon the cover is a quotation from Lenin : " The modern revolution is now entering the period of direct intervention of the oriental races in the destiny of the world."

The Soviet appeal to the Central Asian peasants as descendants of the great Genghiz Khan does not fail to stir their pride or to win their support. This success, however, has not been won without a struggle. Some confused and chaotic years followed the War and the Russian Revolution. Muslim fanaticism and Turkish nationalism spurred the peoples of Central Asia to revolt. The cities of Central Asia—Samarkand and Bukhara, Khiva and Tashkent—were the scene of street fighting, massacre and executions, while the villages of the Zarafshan suffered greatly from drought and famine. When, in 1922, the rising had finally been crushed, the victors had learned to respect their opponents. The Soviet policy towards non-Russian peoples was modified, and the newly created Uzbek and Turcoman Republics were admitted to the Soviet Union on the same basis as the Republics of Russia, the Ukraine, White Russia and Trans-Caucasia. Almost unobserved by Europe another great world empire is being built up. Once more Central Asia is being drawn into the stream of world history.

II.

Early and Medieval Missions in Central Asia

(i.)

AMONG those " devout men from every nation under heaven" who were gathered in Jerusalem on the day of Pentecost were Parthians, Medes and Elamites, who had left their distant homes in Persia and Northern Mesopotamia in order to worship at the

B

Feast. Set on fire by the great experience in which they had shared, they carried the Message to their homes, and thus there arose the " Church of the East," with its headquarters at Edessa in Northern Mesopotamia, and later in Persia.* During the Decian and Diocletian persecutions many Christians living in the Eastern provinces of the Roman Empire fled to Persia and joined themselves to the Church in that country. One hundred and fifty years later this process was repeated by the arrival of the exiled Nestorians.†

The Nestorians brought a new impulse to the Church in Persia ; they were not merely intelligent and industrious workers who would have been welcome to any State, but they were full of glowing missionary zeal. From the fifth century onwards Nestorian Missions had a wonderful period of expansion ; in their own history they were repeating on a larger scale that which happened after the death of Stephen, when " they that were scattered abroad " by persecution " went everywhere preaching the word." The Persian persecutions were most severe, and countless multitudes suffered torture and death rather than deny their Lord. Those who left the country spread in all directions, including the regions of Transoxania and Turkistan ; and wherever they went they carried the Gospel with them.‡

Stimulated by persecution this wonderful missionary activity was also fed and sustained by a deep life of prayer, coupled with a strong emphasis on the study of the Bible. The Nestorian monasteries were practically Missionary Training Schools, in which the chief subject was the study of the Scriptures. The version in com-

---

* Cf. A History of Christian Missions in China. K. S. Latourette, chapter IV.

† I.e., the followers of Nestorius, bishop of Constantinople, (A.D. 428–431) who was condemned and deposed for " heresy " at the Council of Ephesus in 431. " The Nestorians were persecuted with such vigour that they were forced to leave the empire, and by the time of Justinian, A.D. 527, it would have been difficult to find a church within the whole Roman empire that shared the views of Nestorians." For a full treatment of this subject see Nestorian Missionary Enterprise. J. Stewart. T. & T. Clark, 1928.

‡ Nestorian Missionary Enterprise. J. Stewart, p. 9.

mon use was the Peshitto version. The Nestorian missionaries introduced the Syriac alphabet to the Ural-Altaic races of Central Asia.* Some of these students became " solitaries " or " anchorites," giving themselves up chiefly to prayer and intercession. Others remained for a time in the monastery, either continuing their studies, or training those who flocked to them for instruction. Others, taking their lives in their hands, went forth to carry the Gospel to the ends of the earth. They were men of great faith, deeply versed in the Scriptures, large portions of which they knew by heart, fervent in prayer, gentle and humble in manner, and full of love to God and man.

But this spirit of missionary zeal was not the portion merely of a large band of trained men, it animated the whole Church. The sons of Christians " were expected to study the Psalms, the New Testament, and to attend courses of lectures before entering on a business career," and many of the missionary pioneers of Central Asia were artisans, traders, merchants and physicians. Jerome says that " the Huns learn the Psalms from Syrian merchants who burn by the very warmth of their faith."

The golden age of Nestorian Missions in Central Asia lay between the fifth and the ninth centuries. The celebrated memorial in Central China, with its inscription written partly in Syriac, bears the date of February 4th, A.D. 781. On it are the names of the reigning Patriarch, the Bishop of China, of sixty-seven persons who were apparently Western Asiatics, and of sixty-one Chinese Christians, all but two of whom were priests. In the same year (A.D. 781) Timothy, the Nestorian Patriarch, wrote thus to the Maronites of Syria : " The King of the Turks, with nearly all his country, has left his ancient idolatry and has become Christian, and he has requested us in his letter to create a Metropolitan for his country, and this we have done." Writing to another correspondent he says : " In these

---

* Cf. J. Stewart. *Nestorian Missionary Enterprise*. Appendix B. *The Bible of the Nestorians and the Spread of Alphabetic Writing and Culture*, p. 330ff.

days the Holy Spirit has anointed a Metropolitan for the Turks and we are preparing to consecrate another one for the Tibetans."

Vague rumours of these happenings in the East filtered through to Europe and gave rise to the legend of *Prester John* which was so widely diffused throughout the Middle Ages. The occasion of the birth of this legend is interesting as an illustration of Nestorian missionary influence. About the year A.D. 1007 the Metropolitan of Merv wrote to the Nestorian Patriarch to tell him some good news. In the course of his letter he relates how the King of a people called the Keraits (Eastern Turks living near Lake Baikal) was out hunting among the mountains when he was overtaken by a violent snowstorm and lost his way. Just when he was in despair someone appeared and said to him : " If you believe in Christ I will lead you in the right direction, and you will not die here." When the King had reached the tents in safety he summoned some Christian merchants who were there and asked them what he ought to do. They gave him a Gospel and told him he must be baptized. The " good news " in this letter is the fact of the conversion of this King which was speedily followed by a movement in which about two hundred thousand Turks and Mongols became Christians.*

Nestorian Missions in Mongolia, China and Northern Siberia, began rather later than in Transoxania and Turkistan, and they continued until the thirteenth century. By the beginning of the eleventh century the influence of the Nestorian Church extended from China to Mesopotamia and from Lake Baikal to Cape Comorin. Indeed, in the opinion of Dr. Latourette, if the Nestorian Missions had been " supported by powerful Christian monarchs the entire religious map of Central Asia might have been altered." It is no exaggeration to say that this was " the most missionary Church the world has ever seen."

---

* Cf. *A History of Christian Missions in China.*   K. S. Latourette, p. 63ff.

Further, as Dr. John Stewart points out in his inspiring study of Nestorian Missions, " all this was accomplished without any of the elaborate machinery that we have come to look upon as necessary for the carrying on of the missionary work of the twentieth century." He adds some highly suggestive comments on this fact : " If one compares the outcome of the missionary activity of the ' Church of the East ' with the results of the more highly developed organizations of to-day, one may well ask if the missionaries of those early centuries have not, even yet, something to teach us as to the methods and conditions that are essential to the gathering out and building up of a Christian community, which shall not be only self-supporting and self-governing, but, most important of all, self-propagating as well."

Up to this point it is an inspiring story. It is, however, a fact of experience that the vitality of Christianity needs to be constantly renewed. Every generation has to fight the battle of faith afresh. There is no substitute for a living Christian experience, and if this dies out in the Church in any land no strength of organization, custom or tradition, will avail to keep that Church alive. Thus, when towards the end of the sixteenth century some Jesuit missionaries revisited the cities where groups of Nestorian Christians were said to exist, all they could discover were some material relics—a bell, a cross, or a Greek inscription. All other traces had been blotted out.

The causes of this decline seem to have been of two kinds, internal and external.* The slow insidious process

---

* Discussing the parallel problem of the disappearance of Nestorian Christianity from *China*, Dr. Latourette suggests that it was due to the following factors :—

(*a*) Nestorian Christianity was always primarily the faith of a foreign community ;

(*b*) It arrived in China at a time when there was no particular sense of need for a new faith ;

(*c*) The Nestorian missionaries were separated from the centre of their Church by immense distances and could look for little assistance and inspiration from the main body of their fellow-believers.

of internal decay was undoubtedly due to the growth of the spirit of compromise. According to Sir Henry Yule, by the end of the tenth century Christianity in Central Asia had already lost much of its earlier vitality owing to the rise of Manichean and other dualistic cults. It was still more greatly affected by Buddhism. " If Christianity "—says Stewart— " exerted a liberalizing influence on Buddhism, it in turn had a similar effect on Christianity. Evidently there was a levelling up on the one hand and a levelling down on the other. The spirit of compromise was abroad. It was a question of give and take. Not perhaps that there was any formal departure from, or denial of, fundamental doctrines, but less emphasis was probably laid on these than their importance demanded, and the influence of the Nestorians on the non-Christians among whom they lived, and their power to exert a restraining influence on the Mongol storm which was about to burst on Asia, was correspondingly decreased. The note of urgency and definiteness which had been so characteristic of their message in the early centuries had disappeared ; the Laodicean period in their history had set in."*

Thus it came about that a Church, which in its early days had only been stimulated by persecution, was unable to stand against the overwhelming forces of Islam and of the persecutions which accompanied the extension of Islam in Central Asia, and later of the Mongol devastations of the thirteenth century. Under the grandson of Hulagu Khan† all the Christian Churches in his empire were destroyed, and the order was issued that every Christian should be banished from his dominions.

The final blow to Christianity in Central and Northern Asia and in Mongolia was dealt by Tamerlane. He hated the Christians, destroyed their towns,

---

* *Nestorian Missionary Enterprise.* J. Stewart, p. 253.

† Great-nephew of Genghiz Khan, Viceroy of Persia A.D. 1256, said to have been a supporter of the Christian religion. (See *Nestorian Missionary Enterprise*, pp. 268–270, by J. Stewart.)

churches and monasteries, hunted the terror-stricken
refugees out of their dens and caves among the
mountains and massacred them by the thousand.
So great was the terror he created that it has been
said that " his mere nod was sufficient to cause vast
multitudes to abandon Christianity." With the
complete victory of Tamerlane, Islam was firmly
established in Central Asia, while in the lands which
had suffered less severely Buddhism became the chief
religion.*

(ii.)

In the year 1238, Europe was suddenly awakened
to the Mongol danger. Panic seized the minds of men
as they heard of these savage hordes who had " brought
terrible devastation to the eastern parts (of Europe),
laying them waste with fire and carnage." A curious
little incident which has been preserved shows how
widespread was the fear inspired by the Mongol
invasion. In the year 1240, the people of Gothland
and Friesland did not dare to go to Yarmouth for the
herring fishery as usual, in consequence of which it is
recorded that " the herrings were so cheap that forty
or fifty sold for a piece of silver."†

It was at this time, when " distress and darkness
and the gloom of anguish " were brooding over Europe,
that the Christian Church rose up declaring that in
one way only could civilization be saved from doom :
by winning the barbarians for Christ, and through
Christianity to civilization.

Inspired by these motives the first Franciscan
missionaries set out on their adventurous journey to
Asia. Three names stand out among those who
embarked on this courageous campaign : Friar John

---

* *The Churches of Eastern Christendom.* B. J. Kidd, chapter XVI.

† *Contemporaries of Marco Polo :* edited by M. Komroff, Introduction, p. xiii.

de Plano Carpini, Friar William of Rubruck, and, somewhat later, Friar Odoric.*

Carpini set out from Lyons on Easter Day, 1245, on the first important journey made by a European into the vast Mongol Empire. The expedition occupied two years, and involved great hardships. Carpini and his companions often slept on the bare snow, and they suffered much from hunger. Carpini brought back a letter from Kuyuk Khan (grandson of Genghiz Khan) to the Pope, which ends by asking the Pope to come to the East and do homage to the Mongol rulers : " And if you do not observe the order of God . . . then we will know you as our enemy." Carpini did not live long after his return to Europe. Worn out by the hardships he had endured, he died in 1252.

William of Rubruck left Europe for the East the year after Carpini's death. He was sent by King Louis IX of France, who gave him a little money for his journey, letters to the Mongol Khan and a Bible. The story of his journey is vivid and accurate and a valuable record of travel. Rubruck returned to Europe in 1255. The results of his mission were somewhat doubtful, as the Mongol Khan had no real desire to receive the Christian message. Rubruck's references to the " Christians " he met in Central Asia are interesting ; he was often shocked by their ignorance and disgusted by their paganism ; of one group he says : " They were ignorant of all things regarding the Christian religion, excepting only the name of Christ."

Friar Odoric set out for the East about 1318. After a long and hazardous journey by way of India he returned overland through Tibet, Persia, and the land of the famous Assassins.† He died in Italy in 1331. Soon after his death his fame both as saint and traveller spread far and wide.

The Franciscan missions were most successful ;

---

* For the full account of these travellers see *Contemporaries of Marco Polo*. Edited by *M. Komroff*. 1928.

† A Shiite sect which was active in Syria and Persia from the eleventh to the thirteenth century ; it was crushed by Hulagu Khan.

by the close of the thirteenth century they were firmly established in China ; their converts were so numerous that Pope Clement V found it necessary to appoint Asiatic bishops, and in 1307 John de Monte Corvino was consecrated Archbishop of " Cambaluc in Cathay."

Corvino translated the New Testament and the Psalms into the " language most used among the Tartars," and the outlook was promising for the future. His enthusiasm fired other groups of men in the Church, and the authorities began to further the cause of missions in Asia with something of the ardour which Corvino himself possessed. The great pioneer died in 1328, and with his death the best days of the mission to the Far East were over. The Church in Europe, however, did not at first show any signs of failing energy. A certain Brother Nicholas, also a Franciscan, was appointed to succeed Corvino, and he set out for Cathay accompanied by several helpers. It is not known whether he ever reached Peking, but it is recorded that he arrived at Almalig, the modern Kulja (now on the frontier between Russian and Chinese territory), and that in 1338, Pope Benedict XII wrote to the Jagatai Khan thanking him for his courtesy to Brother Nicholas.

Rome did not give up the effort to plant the Faith in Central Asia without a struggle. In the early years of the fourteenth century, for instance, we hear of the establishment of a complete Persian hierarchy with a Metropolitan whose seat was at a town south of the Caspian and whose jurisdiction extended over Persia, India, Ethiopia and Central Asia. Yet before the time of Tamerlane the Roman Missions had lost touch with the governing classes in Central Asia, and by the time he came upon the scene the Islamizing process was almost complete. As late as 1362, however, there were still traces of Roman Catholic missionary effort in Northern Tartary. Probably it was about this time that the Latin Missions in Central Asia were swept away by a fierce storm of persecution.

In the second half of the fourteenth century the great Mongol Empire began to totter ; finally it fell before the incessant attacks of the Chinese. Luxury and the effeminate influences of civilization had so degenerated the Mongol race that its power was gone, and the people were driven from China and other conquered lands back to their own inhospitable uplands, where they finally relapsed into semi-nomadic pastoral life.*

From the time of the reassertion of Celestial supremacy, the ancient policy of isolation, to which the Chinese revert by a dominating psychological instinct, led them to expel the foreign traders who had followed the missionaries, and Islam, which had been temporarily checked by the Mongols, once more closed its fatal grasp on the peoples of Central Asia, where it remains unchallenged to this day.

The number of the missionaries steadily decreased, and, though occasional mention is made of reinforcements, they declined and finally entirely disappeared.†
" They vanished in the gathering darkness and then all is silent."

---

* " In the latter half of the fourteenth century, the Franciscan Mission fell upon evil days. In Europe the Black Death depleted the houses of the Order, and so much energy was required to maintain and replenish them that scant resources were available for the distant and perilous mission to the Far East. More disastrous still was the break-up of the Mongol Empire. As it progressed, the various routes to Cathay became unsafe. Fresh invasions, such as those of Timur, wasted Eastern and Central Asia. Missionaries were martyred in Central Asia."—*A History of Christian Missions in China.* K. S. Latourette, p. 73.

† *Cf.* " Of one thing we may be certain : the Chinese national reaction which broke out in 1368 set the Ming dynasty upon the throne, and expelled the Mongol Yuen, put an end for centuries to Western Christianity and to European trade within the Middle Kingdom. When this calamity befell, it is said that the friars flying across Asia from Peking to Sarai and the Volga, carried with them the relics of the Grand Khan converted by Corvino."—*Encyclopaedia of Religion and Ethics,* Vol. VIII, p. 711.

(iii)

Early in the sixteenth century the Portuguese, landing on the east coast of Asia, became familiar with the name of Peking without being aware that it was identical with the great city of Cambaluc whose name was famous to all educated Westerners. Gradually it became evident that though the names were different, yet the description of the people, customs, products and trade, tallied perfectly with that which the ancient Franciscan missionaries gave of Cambaluc. In particular, the renowned Matthew Ricci, who reached Peking in 1598, became convinced of the identity of China with Cathay, of Cambaluc with Peking. His arguments, however, did not meet with universal assent, and the question remained an open one until it was finally settled by Bento de Goes.

Jerome Xavier, missionary at Lahore in 1595, relates that at Akbar's court there was admitted one day to the presence of the Great Mogul a Muhammadan merchant. He stated that he had come from Cathay and had lived in Cambaluc for thirteen years. He said that many in Cathay were " followers of Jesus," and that there were also many " followers of Moses," as well as Muhammadans.

The upshot of this remarkable audience was that Bento de Goes, a lay brother of the Jesuit order, set out on a great adventure : the endeavour to reach Cathay by the overland route, through the dangerous Muslim lands of Central Asia. In order to escape notice he let his hair and beard grow, and adopted the dress of a Persian trader. De Goes started out from India in 1603. He travelled through Afghanistan and the Pamirs, visiting Yarkand, Khotan and Aksu on the way. At last in the winter of 1605 he reached the Great Wall of China, and entered the town of Suchow, in Kansu. " This admirable person," as Sir Henry Yule calls him, spent some time in Suchow ; finally he died there in March, 1607 ; in the words of the old chronicler, " seeking Cathay he found Heaven." Before his death, however, he had established communication with Ricci at Peking, and had proved that Cathay and China were one and the same country.

*   *   *   *   *

From the beginning of the seventeenth century no more was heard of Central Asia in the Christian West. So far as Christian missions were concerned this vast region had ceased to exist.

The Situation in
Central Asia To-day

CHAPTER I.

Russian Central Asia

THE TURCOMAN, UZBEK AND KAZAK REPUBLICS

I.

SPRING has come to Samarkand. The spreading silver poplars with their over-arching branches throw a welcome shade over the wide European roads, hiding the houses so successfully that it seems almost impossible to believe that one is in the famous city of " Golden Samarkand." Every street is an avenue of willow, acacia, elm and poplar trees, all clothed in their fresh green leaves. The atmosphere is so clear and translucent that every atom of dust shines with a golden radiance.

Samarkand lies on a high plain, bounded on the south by a jagged wall of snowy mountains. The Asiatic quarter with its mosques and schools lies upon a patch of uneven ground ; the whole is dominated by an old fortress. There, amid an Oriental mingling of squalor and beauty, the real life of the city goes on. Yet at every step one may " kick a fragment of the past." In the Afrosiab quarter the ground is honey-combed with holes where men have been searching for coins or unbroken relics, or the pariah dogs have been hunting for bones. All around are the ruins of ancient buildings, chief among them the magnificent Bibi-Khanum, whose tiles of brilliant blue still glow in undimmed splendour on crumbling domes.

Autumn is the bracing season in Samarkand The trees turn yellow ; the air is keen. Then comes December with its clear cold days. Through the leafless branches hidden houses emerge from their summer seclusion, while far away across the flat plain the snow mountains stand out clearly against the deep blue sky.

Samarkand is full of memories of the past. Here Alexander slew Clytus. Here Genghiz Khan quartered his armies. Here, above all, Tamerlane has left his mark. Samarkand was the city of his dreams. He found it a half-ruined town of mud and brick and wood ; he rebuilt it and turned it into the " Rome of Asia." Blue was the favourite colour of the Tartars, and Timur's new buildings shone with façades of turquoise. The fame of Samarkand spread through Asia, and everywhere it was known as Gok-kand, the Blue City.

Bukhara is very different from Samarkand : " One has the money, the other the charm." It is a crowded huckstering place, with some of the fascination of the Middle Ages still clinging to its closely-packed houses and narrow lanes. The bazaar is wonderful, with its dim passages pierced here and there by shafts of sunlight, with its noise and its smells, odours of mutton fat and camels and men, mingling with the fragrance of nutmeg and cinnamon and Oriental spices. Nine-tenths of the people who jostle each other in these crowded alleys wear the same kind of white turban, forming a beautiful and harmonious background to the riot of colour on the stalls with their flaming silks, jewellery, carpets, and sparkling objects of tin or glass. It has been well said that " the glory of Holy Bukhara is her bazaar."

Both Samarkand and Bukhara depend for their very existence upon one of the famous rivers of Turkistan, the Zarafshan, the Polytimetus of the ancients, known now-a-days as the " Strewer of Gold," the " Picture of Life." Rising in the Alai Mountains, it runs through a ravine for two hundred miles, then for another two hundred miles through open country ; finally, it loses itself in the plains without reaching the Oxus.

Thus we see clearly why it is that the scattered population of Russian Central Asia lives in the fertile oases which " seem to float like islands upon a sea of sand." The soil is so fruitful that the inhabitants are able to supply almost all their wants from the produce of their fields and gardens.

When Sir Percy Sykes was travelling to Kashgar in 1915, he passed through Russian Central Asia. His sister gives some delightful impressions of their journey. Here are two glimpses on the road between Andijan and Osh. It was springtime, and as they drove along she noticed that " ploughing was in full swing, barley some inches high in the fields, fruit blossom everywhere, and the poplars and willows planted along the countless irrigation channels made a delicate veil of pale green. Beyond the cultivation lay bare rolling hills, behind which rose the lofty mountain ranges which we must cross before we could reach our destination.

" The whole country seemed thickly populated, and we passed through village after village teeming with life, the source of which is the river. . . . Tortoises were emerging from their winter seclusion, the croak of the frog filled the land, hoopoes and the pretty doves, which are semi-sacred and never molested, flew about, and the ringing cry of quail and partridge sounded from cages in which the birds were kept as pets. . . . Our second day's march found us approaching the mountains, and we rode to the top of a low pass where hills slashed with scarlet, crimson and yellow, rose one behind another, to be dominated by the glorious snow-covered Tien Shan peaks, clear cut against a superb blue sky."

The further they travelled towards Chinese Turkistan, the more barren became the country, until they wondered how the flocks and herds could subsist upon such scanty vegetation. " At one point the hills were a bright scarlet, and it was strange to see a red mud-built village with sheep grazing in this brilliantly coloured setting."*

Away to the north and west the sands of Russian Central Asia merge into the great Kirghiz Steppe, the original home of the Turks and the Mongols, " the mother of nations and of conquerors." When Kublai Khan was at the height of his power, he enclosed

---

* *Through Deserts and Oases of Central Asia :* P. and E. Sykes, pp. 22–29.

C

within his palace grounds a little field which he sowed with grasses from the prairie, in order that, as he put it, " his children might remember and be humble before the mother of them all."

Kipchak, " emptiness, space," is the Kirghiz name for these vast grassy plains which stretch away and away in every direction like some great sea of land. In summer they lie drab, scorched and withered beneath the blazing sun ; sometimes even the sparse grey grass disappears before a greater desolation, and the steppe flowers only with the white bones of worn-out sheep and camels, recalling the Kirghiz saying : " The steppe is cruel and Heaven is far." But in the springtime the steppe is transformed ; the grass springs up afresh, the few dwarf trees and bushes burst into leaf, and the lovely tulip of the steppe sparkles on the green turf, and sways to and fro at the touch of the light airs of spring. The " empty " steppe has become *Eulnek*, a " flowering meadow."

Between the Sea of Aral—that strange expanse of inland ocean with its ships and seamen, and its mysterious islands—and Lake Balkhash, the steppe is strewn with lakes and tarns, " strung together like pearls on a string."

The only signs of human life in the steppe country are the round black tents of the nomads, and it was in such surroundings that Genghiz Khan was born.

It is a vast country, this region of Russian Central Asia, stretching from the shores of the Caspian Sea to the great snow mountains on the borders of Sinkiang, and from Siberia to Afghanistan.

II.

Russia was an Asiatic power before her position in Europe was established, but the Russian advance into Central Asia belongs to the nineteenth century. By the end of the eighteenth century Russia had formed an irregular frontier, twelve hundred miles in length, across the Kirghiz Steppes. This desert borderland was a constant source of trouble. Russian statesmen, therefore, determined to try to stabilize conditions in Turkistan. This movement began in the early thirties of last century ; at first progress was slow, and success was not finally assured until the Russians captured Merv and reached the great Hindu Kush mountain borderland in 1884. The stages of the Russian advance south of the frontier line of 1846 are clear : Tashkent was occupied in 1865, Samarkand in 1868, Khiva, the Oxus and Trans-Caspian Provinces in 1873, Akhal Tekke in 1881, Merv in 1884 and the Pamirs in 1895. Fifty years of political restlessness and fever were ended by the Anglo-Russian Convention of 31st August, 1907, which dealt with Persia, Afghanistan and Tibet.

The Russian Government consolidated its position in Central Asia by opening up trade routes, and linking up the most important towns by railway. For many years the Russian Government gave peace, protection, and a certain measure of prosperity to the people of Turkistan. As a colonizing experiment, however, the Russian administration of Central Asia during the nineteenth century can scarcely be called a success.

The upheaval of the World War stirred up a spirit of restlessness in Russian Turkistan. Even before the Russian Revolution of 1917 local risings occurred in which Austrian and Hungarian prisoners of war took part.

In 1920, an organized insurrection broke out, known as the " Basmaji* Revolt," which assumed large proportions. Two main causes led to this revolt. On the one hand, the fanatical Muslims of Turkistan had been goaded to fury by the blasphemous propaganda and the policy of confiscation of ecclesiastical property carried on by the Soviets ; on the other hand, there was the growing force of Turkish nationalism, which presented a sharp challenge to the Bolshevists' idea of " Eurasian " domination. Enver Pasha, the Turkish Nationalist, appeared in Bukhara in November,

---

* Literally " robber," really " rebel." *Cf.* " Badmashi."

1921, and organized an anti-Soviet pan-Turanian movement, by which he hoped to combine into one huge Islamic State the Turks from Angora eastward including Afghanistan.

In January, 1922, Enver sent an ultimatum to Moscow demanding a total evacuation of Turkistan by the Soviet Government. In answer the Red Army was despatched to Bukhara, and in August the movement was definitely broken by the death of Enver Pasha in a rearguard action. The two Emirates were then turned into two independent Soviet Republics.* The significance of these happenings has scarcely been realized in Europe, yet, to quote Sir Denison Ross, " Things have come very near to the creation of another big Empire where so many big Empires have been set up in the past."

Before the Russian Revolution the term " Russian Turkistan " was used in a very wide sense. At the present time, however, it is limited to the region which is covered by the Turcoman and Uzbek Socialist Soviet Republics. Both are constituent states of the U.S.S.R. Economically, the new organization centres in the Uzbek Republic, " upon which the other units are dependent, while this state is entirely dependent upon Soviet Russia—the sole consumer of its cotton. In this way the whole vast territories of the Kirghiz Steppes and Turkistan have become economic feeders of Soviet Russia."† The official name of the Steppe region which lies to the north of the old Russian Turkistan is the *Cossack Autonomous Socialist Soviet Republic*, or *Kazakstan*.

Soviet rule in Central Asia is characterized by energy, intelligence and industry. Coal, oil, cotton and silk are all being produced, and roads and railways are being improved and extended. The Turkistan-Siberian railway, which was begun in 1927, is to be completed in 1931. The northern section of the railway

---

* The " Basmaji " bands continued to give trouble until 1926, and in 1929 they renewed their activities.

† *Europe and the East* : N. D. Harris, p. 467.

was inaugurated on 15th December, 1928. An extensive re-organization of the Air Service in these republics is being planned. At the present time Khiva and Dyushambe in Tadzhikstan are connected by aeroplane. Very soon, however, the Government expects to open a new route from Tashkent and Samarkand to Dyushambe. The flight from Tashkent to Dyushambe will occupy six hours ; at present it takes seven days to cover the same distance by railway or motor-car.

These separate ethnic republics enjoy a considerable degree of autonomy. Each one has its own schools and school-books, and various Turkish dialects which have not hitherto been reduced to writing are now being studied by educational specialists.

The main policy directing these Muslim republics lies in the hands of Moscow, but to a considerable extent they are allowed to manage their own home affairs. It is noteworthy that they have become far more aware of Europe than Europe is aware of them. News, not only of the Eastern but of the Western world, is here transmitted by word of mouth, and it is remarkable how sensitive these remote people are to world movements. A carelessly uttered word by European politicians may soon be the talk of the market place in many a town of Russian Central Asia.

III.

The region of Russian influence in Central Asia has been the scene of so many migrations and conquests that the population is naturally extremely mixed. The predominant element is the Ural-Altaic, and the following are the chief tribes.

The *Turkomans* were nomad horse-breeders until the Russian occupation of Merv. In 1881, the Russians destroyed their power by capturing their chief fortress and putting down their slave trade. The " clan " spirit is strong among them, and they seem to be a fairly democratic people.

The *Uzbeks* are of Turko-Tartar origin, but their

contact with Persians, Kirghiz and Mongols, has been frequent and intimate. The Turkish element is probably predominant, though in the case of the Uzbeks of Khiva the Iranian type is uppermost. On the whole, women are better treated among the Uzbeks than among the Sarts and Tadzhiks.

The *Sarts* are Uzbeks who have settled down and given up a nomad life. They occupy themselves with trade, and less often with agriculture. They all speak Turkish and are Sunnite Muslims; there are many Sûfîs among them.

Of smaller groups there are the *Dzungaris*, the *Kalmuks* and the *Torgutes*. The *Tadzhiks* (Aryans) who inhabit the little " Autonomous Socialist Soviet Republic " of *Tadzhikstan* live under the wing of Uzbekistan. These people form the intellectual element in the country; they are the chief owners of the irrigated lands, merchants and mullahs. They are Sunnite Muslims.

The *Kirghiz* are divided into two branches : (1) the *Kazak* (Cossack)* Kirghiz, and (2) the *Kara* (Black) Kirghiz. These tribes are virtually the masters of the steppes and the highlands. They have been described as " a gross and stolid people, kindly, but given to fits of sullen rage that know no bounds, black and violent as the desert storms. They are superstitious, but not religious, their only real faith is a vague pantheism. Their lives are centred about their flocks, their horses and their herds, and their minds are the minds of herdsmen."

IV.

Jalāl al-Dīn Rumi,† the great Persian poet, wrote in one of his poems :
 " Thou wilt to Bukhara ? O fool for thy pains ! Thither thou goest, to be put into chains."

---

* Literally, Free Birds of the Steppe.

† Born A.D. 1207 in Eastern Persia. Died A.D. 1273 at Qōniya (Iconium) in Anatolia.

And Arminius Vambéry* says that he found exactly
the same feeling about the Muslims of Turkistan
among his learned friends in Turkey and Persia.
They warned him of his danger when he announced
his intention of going to Bukhara and Samarkand,
and when he returned and described his experiences
many of them criticized and laughed at " the over-
heated religious zeal of their fellow-believers." From
various causes this part of Central Asia has long been
a stronghold of Islam, to the point of fanaticism.
Hence the boast : " Bukhara is the real strength of
Islam."

In the opinion of Professor Vambéry this boast is
fully supported by facts. He considers that Bukhara
is the main stronghold of Islam for the whole of Central
Asia. It is the social capital, and the centre of Muslim
culture for this vast region. It contains several colleges
and schools for the training of Muslim teachers.
Kokand, Samarkand and Tashkent, are also important
Islamic centres. The Muslim press is fairly active in
these towns. Tashkent has five Muslim newspapers,
Kokand and Samarkand one each, and papers are
printed at Bukhara in the Arabic, Persian and Turki
languages.†

To-day ninety-five per cent. of the population
profess Islam, and this faith inspires and regulates
the religious and social life of the people. The smallest
village has its mosque, to which is attached the school
and the shelter for the poor and the pilgrim. The
strength of Islam, therefore, is the first difficulty
which would confront the Christian missionary. The
second is the closed door of the Soviet Government.
So far only a few missionaries have lived in Russian
Central Asia. Eighteen years ago two members of the
Swedish Missionary Society were sent to Bukhara,
but they were only allowed to remain for a short time.
At one time the German Mennonites started work
amongst the Kirghiz : one of these missionaries acted
as agent for the British and Foreign Bible Society at

---

* Born A.D. 1832.
† Cf. *Across the World of Islam* : S. M. Zwemer : p. 309.

Tashkent until 1917, when, owing to the War, this mission had to give up its work. Individual Christians from other lands have done quiet work amongst the people, but under the rule of Soviet Russia even they have had to leave the country.

For generations the Scriptures in *Russian* have been finding their way across the border. For Russian Central Asia itself, the British and Foreign Bible Society has published the four Gospels in *Uzbek*, the *lingua franca* of the districts round Bukhara, Khiva and Kokand. The translation was made by an inspector of schools who was editor of a newspaper in Tashkent. The latest edition is dated 1913. Other names by which Uzbek is also known are *Sart*, *Turkestani* and *Central Asian Turkish*. Remembering the importance of Bukhara as a great centre of intellectual life, as well as of busy trade, it is important to note that the Gospels are available in its own form of speech.

In *Jagatai* or *Trans-Caspian Turkish*, sometimes known as *Eastern Turki*, or as *Tekke Turkoman*, the British and Foreign Bible Society has printed the Gospel of St. Matthew for the tribe of nomads found in the oasis to the north of Damani Koh and the Gulistan Mountains, and the deserts as far as the Oxus. They are said to number anything from two hundred thousand to five hundred thousand.

Meanwhile, however, while the door to Russian Central Asia is bolted against the foreign missionary, a spontaneous Russian movement has been springing up. The possibilities for evangelistic work are much greater in these remote regions than in Soviet Russia itself. These Russian Christians go " everywhere, preaching the Word," both to their fellow-countrymen, and to the peoples of the Turcoman, Uzbek and Kazak Republics. In a large number of towns and villages little communities of Christians have already been formed.* The Bible is being read with eagerness ;

---

* Further details of this movement can be obtained, if desired, from the World Dominion Press.

indeed, at present it is impossible to keep pace with the demand for it, especially for translations in the various languages and dialects of the country. This movement is strong in the Russian Altai region, whence its leaders hope to send a constant stream of missionaries throughout Russian Central Asia. This widespread evangelical movement breathes something of the fragrance of primitive Christianity, when " the disciples were filled with joy and with the Holy Ghost."

CHAPTER II.

Chinese Turkistan (Sinkiang)

I.

HIGH mountains surround the vast plain of Sinkiang. It is a desert land, fringed by oases. Much of the country is covered by great sandy wastes, where the sand is piled up by the force of the wind into fantastic dunes ; other regions are bare and stony, and in some parts are wide rolling steppes covered with coarse grass. Hemmed in on three sides by lofty mountain ranges, and on the fourth by a great desert, Sinkiang is indeed remote from the world : " It is a land steeped in the Middle Ages, picturesque and quaint almost beyond belief."

The land is crossed by a few ancient trade routes which connect oases of varying size and importance.* Some of them contain only one well or spring of very brackish water, others consist of hamlets with a few acres of cultivated fields, while in some cases large walled cities are surrounded by thousands of acres of highly irrigated fertile land.

In springtime these oases are most attractive. The trees that border the numerous irrigation channels are delicately flushed with green ; the Babylonian willows are bursting into fragrant bloom ; the flat fields are a brilliant carpet of springing corn. Flowers are few, but the graveyards are filled with sheets of blue iris, and here and there by the sandy bridle-tracks bushes of wild roses fill the air with their perfume. Fruit trees abound, and the low mud houses are embowered in masses of the pink and white blossom of apple and peach and pear.

---

* It is estimated that the area of the oases is rather less than one and a half per cent. of the whole country. The Chinese, however, claim that thirty per cent. of the land is under cultivation, thirty per cent. consists of mountains and lakes, and forty per cent. is desert.

The great drawback to spring in Chinese Turkistan is the frequency of the sandstorms which rage furiously at times, filling the air with a constant haze of dust. In the Kashgar Oasis, for instance, it is said that there are only one hundred clear days in the year. The Kashgaris, however, do not complain, for they are glad of the relief from the brilliant sunshine. This haze gives the sunsets of Kashgar a peculiar charm. The sky will be softly flushed with pale yellow and mauve and rose-colour, while the whole scene is bathed in a wonderful golden light.

Rivers are scarce, for, owing to the sandy nature of the soil, the water produced by the melting snows buries itself in the sand as soon as it has reached the foot of such ranges as the Barkul Mountains and the Tien Shan. The Yarkand or Tarim River, which takes its rise in the mountain ranges to the south-west, is the largest in the province, and the principal cities of Sinkiang are to be found along its bank. The Manas River, in the north-east, waters an area which is the granary of Eastern Turkistan.

Urumtsi,* the capital, is a rapidly growing city, and during the last few years the Russian Quarter has gained in importance. Its population is cosmopolitan, and the provincial Governor appointed by the Central Government has his residence here. His jurisdiction extends from the borders of China proper to Siberia and Kashgaria.

Manas, further north, is situated on the river of the same name, and is a market town in the centre of the best-watered farming country of the northern area.

The great oasis of Hami, which the Turks call Kumul, stands at the cross-roads of the trade routes stretching north, south, east and west.

Kucheng, east of Urumtsi, is a commercial centre which draws Chinese from all the different provinces to its business firms.

---

* Known to the Chinese as Tihwafu, or by its local name of Hungmiao-tze.

Barkul occupies a unique position behind the snow-clad range of the same name and on the borders of the Barkul Lake.

Turfan lies in a depression below sea level. The locality is very fertile, and Turfan grows enough grapes to supply the whole province with sultanas.

Khotan supplies the white jade or nephrite which Chinese craftsmen have carved so beautifully that it has gained world-wide repute.

In the south-west are Kashgar and Yarkand. Kashgar is a town of such political importance that it needs the consular representation of Western lands. It is the terminus of the Trans-Himalayan caravan routes connecting India with Central Asia.

II.

After many vicissitudes this Central Province of Asia was finally brought under Chinese control in the eighteenth century, and it has gradually become one of China's most valuable colonies.

At the fall of the Manchu dynasty, in 1911, its Governor was a Manchu, but at the time of crisis he fled. There was a period of fighting in which the Muslim troops took a prominent part, and their leader, General Ma, gave his support to a Chinese official who had held various appointments in Kansu and in Sinkiang, and who declared himself to be whole-heartedly on the Republican side.

Once having been entrusted with the reins of Government, Governor Yang showed himself to be a firm and able ruler. His appointment was later confirmed by the central Government at Peking, and he was able to keep his territory free from the disturbances and civil war which have torn the provinces of China proper.

His methods were those of a Dictator. He allowed no newspaper to be published in his province ; even the circulation of Chinese papers was forbidden. The cultivation of the opium poppy was absolutely prohibited, and brigandage was held in check. An effective system of espionage and censorship was exercised, and summary punishment was meted out to those who were suspected of disloyalty.

A ruler so autocratic and ruthless as Governor Yang was bound to rouse bitter hostility against himself. Suddenly, the smouldering hatred flared up, and, on 7th July, 1928, while Yang was giving away the prizes at the Russian School of Law and Politics in Urumtsi, he was assassinated by the bodyguard of the Minister of Foreign Affairs.

The Foreign Minister himself and his bodyguard of thirty soldiers were immediately captured by the Minister of the Interior, named Ching Shu-jen, the adopted son of Yang Tsen-hsin. The Foreign Minister was tried by court martial and shot. Two days after the death of Yang, Ching took over the government of the Province. The death of Governor Yang will cause great changes. It is even possible that these changes may be so drastic and far-reaching that they will alter the course of Central Asian history.

A glance at the map will show how deeply Russian interests are involved in the future of Chinese Turkistan. Russia controls the only two feasible routes into Sinkiang : (1) the route to Urumtsi from Omsk on the Trans-Siberian railway, via Semipalatinsk ; by this route the journey from London, by rail and road, takes forty-five days ; (2) the route to Urumtsi by the Trans-Caspian railway, via Osh and Kashgar ; by this route the whole distance from London to Urumtsi can be covered in about eighty-six days.

Sinkiang has recently added to its territory the triangular area north of Urumtsi which was previously part of Outer Mongolia ; this brings the frontier of Sinkiang into touch with that of Soviet Russia, and throws it open more than ever to penetration from that side. There seems little doubt that Russia has designs on the territories of Mongolia, Manchuria and Sinkiang which the present weakness of China greatly facilitates.

It is impossible to foretell what course events will take, but the political future of Chinese Turkistan is fraught with perilous possibilities.

III.

The people of Chinese Turkistan represent many tribes and nations, diverse in type, manners, customs and religion. Some are Aryans, others belong to races of Ural-Altaic stock, and some are of mixed blood. The following is a brief description of the tribes which make up the population.

The *Turkis*, who are also called Chan-tou, are the agriculturists of the fertile oases, and their caravans carry the produce of one part of the country to the other. They are known ethnologically as Turanian Turks. Their language is Turki, and they are a Muslim people.

The *Kazaks* are a tent-dwelling people distributed over the steppes of Northern Dzungaria. There is reason for believing them to be descended from bands of people who, in the thirteenth and fourteenth centuries, reverted to a nomadic life in order to escape from the strong state organization of the Turkic empires. The conditions of life which they adopted have led to their mixing freely with nomads like the Western Mongols. They are Muslims, but they are less fanatical than the Turkis.

The *Tungans* are a Chinese-speaking people of a Semitic type of countenance, probably of Arab descent. Being Muslims they do not mix easily with the Chinese, and at times of rebellion they usually play a leading part.

The *Taranchis* (farmers), or Ili Tartars, are to be found in the Kulja district of Ili. As their name indicates, they are an agricultural people, a large number of whom emigrated to Russian Turkistan at the time that Kulja passed under Chinese rule. They are Muslims.

The *Sarts* (town-dwellers) really belong to Russian

Central Asia, but they appear sporadically in Sinkiang. They congregate in village centres, and although they are chiefly engaged in commerce they are also successful agriculturists. They are reputed to be the best cultivators of cotton and fruit plantations. They are Muslims and keep their women more strictly in seclusion than is usual in other Turki tribes.

The *Nogais* are Tartars, descendants of a tribe which derives its name from an early tribal chief who led his hordes into Europe, whence they returned with many Western women. They are somewhat European in type, and have considerable commercial intercourse with Russia. The Nogais are Muslims, but some of them seem to differ from the Russian colonists solely in the matter of religion.

The *Kirghiz* are a tent-dwelling people living between Aksu and Uch-Turfan. Their occupation is cattle-breeding. In religion they are Muslims.

The *Badakshan* border tribes, who bring tribute to the Governor at Urumtsi, live on the Afghan frontier.

Further, the traders, craftsmen, and market-gardeners, are mainly *Chinese colonists* from the eighteen provinces of China ; their religion is Buddhism. Then there are the *Manchus*, descendants of the Manchu troops which fought under Chien Lung for the conquest of Sinkiang, and who were rewarded for their pains by grants of territory. They are met with in Kulja and on the Siberian border at Chuguchak. Many of them are well educated and are merchants or officials ; they are Buddhists.

Finally, there are the *Mongols*, who belong to the Kalmuk or West Mongolian tribe ; they are a semi-nomadic people whose encampments are found in Karashar, Ili and the Altai Mountains. They are divided into Torgut and Hoshut branches. Their chief occupation is cattle ranging. They are Buddhists, and under the control of Lamas.

The difficulty of governing a province in which so many tribes and nations mingle and where the diversity of race and religion inevitably causes friction, will be easily understood. On the whole, however, the people are attractive, peaceable and tolerant. Further, it must always be remembered that the trade routes of Sinkiang unite India, Russia, Tibet and China, thus bringing this province into a position of political importance which can scarcely be over-estimated.

With very little adjustment the roads of Central Asia could become military highways for motor transport ; wireless communication has already been established between Kashgar and Urga, via Urumtsi.

IV.

To the student of the history of Christian missions it will be a matter of regret that a country so rich in opportunity as Sinkiang has remained until the present time so largely unevangelized. The total missionary force resolves itself into a small group of members of the *Swedish Missionary Society* in Kashgar and three neighbouring towns, and three men, members of the *China Inland Mission*, at Urumtsi. In the year 1908, Mr. George Hunter travelled from Kansu to Urumtsi, where he established his headquarters ; later on he was joined by Mr. Percy Mather and, more recently, by Mr. H. F. Ridley. From this base constant journeys have been made along all the main trade routes. The difficulty of the work can be judged from the fact that there are still only eight communicants.

Some idea of the distances which have been covered may be gathered from the length of journeys which have been made over and over again.* Messrs. Hunter and Mather have not only taken these extensive journeys, but they have also done much valuable

---

* Urumtsi to Kashgar .. .. 56 days' march.

Urumtsi to Ili and Kulja	..	20	,,	,,
Urumtsi to Chuguchak	..	20	,,	,,
Urumtsi to Karashar ..	..	10	,,	,,
Urumtsi to Turfan	..	6	,,	,,
Urumtsi to Hami	..	18	,,	,,
Urumtsi to Barkul	..	18	,,	,,
Urumtsi to Zaisan	..	28	,,	,,
Urumtsi to Kobdo in Altai	..	28	,,	,,

translation into the languages of the peoples among whom they live.

The missionaries of the Swedish Mission reached Sinkiang in 1894. They found almost the entire population professing a form of Muhammadanism which was mixed to a great extent with Indian mysticism and crude superstition. The Mission started work at Kashgar, and in spite of the fact that the country was under the Chinese, its missionaries met with opposition and persecution. At one time the Chinese stirred up the Kashgaris to besiege the little community in the mission house, and afterwards they used every kind of threat to induce the missionaries to leave the district. They stood firm, however, and in the end the Chinese official who was responsible for the trouble was recalled.

The Swedish Mission has now extended its work through the Kashgar Oasis to Hancheng and Yangi-Hessar. Hancheng, a Chinese city, is situated at a distance of seven miles from Kashgar. Yangi-Hessar is a small walled town surrounded by gardens and cultivated land. It stands on the banks of a river bordered by picturesque cliffs, from which there is a fine view of the magnificent range of Muztagh Ata, with its snow-peaks clearly outlined against the blue sky.

A vast marshy plain covered with reeds, varied by stretches of gravelly desert, separates the Kashgar Oasis from that of Yarkand where the Swedish Mission has also founded a station. The Yarkandis are apathetic and dull compared with the lively cheerful Kashgaris, but the reason is obvious : goitre is prevalent ; indeed, it is authoritatively stated that about fifty per cent. of the population are victims of this complaint which here assumes most distressing forms. Yarkand is a dirty, dusty, squalid city. The Swedish missionaries are training boys and girls to cleaner, healthier habits in two orphanages in which are twenty-eight boys and eighteen girls.

The Mission has primary schools in all its stations, and Bible training is given in connection with them.

D

In Kashgar there are two lower primary schools, one for Turki-speaking and one for Chinese-speaking children. In Hancheng there are three schools, one lower primary and one higher primary for boys, and one for girls, all for Chinese-speaking children. In Yangi-Hessar there is one school for Turki-speaking children. In Yarkand there are three schools for Turki-speaking children, one in the station and one in each of the orphanages. In connection with the boys' orphanage there is a training school for workers, and a similar training class is carried on in the evenings at Hancheng for Chinese workers. Sunday schools are connected with all the day schools.

In a few of the larger towns the Chinese have begun to provide schools, but most of the educational work is still being done in connection with the Muhammadan mosques, which number over a thousand, and where the teaching provided is extremely poor. One of the earliest activities of the Swedish Mission was to set up a printing-press, at Kashgar, the first in Sinkiang, from which the missionaries issue books for the use of schools throughout the province. Tracts, hymnbooks, and portions of Scripture are printed in the Eastern Turki dialect. About five thousand tracts and five hundred Gospel portions are distributed annually. At present the total staff of the Swedish Mission is thirty-one, of whom about eight are usually on furlough. There is not a single doctor on the staff, but two missionaries have taken a course at Livingstone College, and there are eight trained nurses. It is therefore surprising that in the year 1926 the attendances at the mission dispensaries were 28,050, of which 15,965 were in Kashgar alone. This work is steadily increasing.

The Swedish Mission is holding on firmly, but it finds it necessary to work quietly and unobtrusively. The Chinese authorities are friendly to the work, but in their desire to keep the peace between Bolshevik influence on the one side, and a disturbed China on the other, they are naturally afraid of any effort which might anger the Mullahs and stir up unrest among the people.   In spite of difficulties and persecutions, chiefly from the Muhammadans, the Church is gradually being built up, and there are several Turki preachers. The dispensary work is of great value in various ways, and in times of tension and danger it is " like a shield." Pioneer work of this nature urgently requires the services of a missionary doctor.

The influence of the Bible is silently and surely making itself felt in Sinkiang, and Scriptures in many languages are available for this region.   China Inland Mission missionaries have reported that they have sold British and Foreign Bible Society Scriptures in about a score of languages in their travels.   Mr. G. W. Hunter, of Urumtsi, has made a great contribution in the translation of the Gospels and of the Acts of the Apostles in the *Kazak* or *Altai* form of Kirghiz, spoken over a wide area from Urumtsi.   He wrote out these versions in Arabic characters.   These sheets were then photographed, and the books were published from the Shanghai Depôt of the British and Foreign Bible Society.   In 1928 over five thousand portions were actually sold in *Kazak*.   The China Inland Mission missionaries and other workers have also distributed books in many other languages : in several forms of *Chinese*, in *Manchu*, *Kashgar Turkish*, *Mongolian*, *Kalmuk*, *Tibetan*, *Arabic*, *Russian* and even in *Nogai* or *Tartar Turkish*.   Indeed, so important did Mr. Hunter find this last-named tongue that he prepared a fresh translation in the dialect used in the two Turkistans and Siberia, especially in the large towns from Urumtsi to Kalgan.   These books were issued in 1925.

In the south-west corner of Sinkiang, in the country round Kashgar, the predominant language is a form of Turkish known as *Kashgar Turkish*.   The whole of the New Testament, and, in addition, Genesis, 1 Samuel and Job, have been issued in this language. Most of these translations were made by members of the lonely advance guard of the Swedish Mission. Others were prepared by Mr. G. W. Hunter, the Rev.

G. Raquette, and the Rev. Johannes Avetaranian, who was at one time a Muslim Turkish mullah.

The *National Bible Society of Scotland* bears the cost of the Arabic Gospels which the Swedish Mission distributes among the mullahs of Kashgar, who refuse to read the Gospels in Turki. They are quite willing to read the Arabic Gospels, and will discuss their contents with the missionaries.

Sinkiang used to be divided into four Tao or circuits, but it is now divided into eight. The Swedish Mission is working in one and has prospect of maintaining the work in two more of these huge districts. At the present time, however, the Kashgar circuit alone is adequately occupied. It is hoped to open stations in the Khotan circuit and the Aksu circuit in the near future. The Urumtsi circuit is occupied by the China Inland Mission. Thus only two circuits are occupied. There remains a vast field for extension of present work and for the evangelistic efforts of the Chinese Christian Church. If the example of Dr. Kao in Kansu could be followed in this vast colony, great things might be achieved.*

Here is a great challenge to the Christian Church, that by its faith and prayer it may call forth labourers into this " harvest." All honour is due to the brave pioneers who labour in these territories in such difficult conditions and who, in spite of almost unbelievable obstacles, persevere in faith and labour in love for the redemption of these peoples.

---

* See page 56ff.

CHAPTER III.

North-West Kansu

I.

FOR centuries Kansu has been one of the "battlefields of humanity." Silent and deserted villages, ruined homes, houses with the air of fortresses, fortified towns, "backed by castles, towers, and signalling posts": these are the sights that greet the traveller along the famous Silk Route between the cities of Lanchow and Liangchow.

Liangchow itself lies on a wide plain. The flat-roofed villages, surrounded by trees bared of branches almost to the top, the feudal castles, and the over-arching cloudless sky, all unite to give the impression of a desert scene in some other part of Asia.

The Province of Kansu is the extreme north-western province of China. Otherwise compact in form, it throws out a narrow arm of territory between Mongolia and Tibet. Scientists have agreed that geographically and ethnologically all that lies beyond the city of Liangchow should be reckoned as part of Central Asia rather than of China proper.

The traveller cannot fail to be impressed by the change of conditions which he meets at this point. The land is traversed by one main road which lies almost at the foot of the Tibetan hills, and within sight of the Mongolian sands. The natural course of the rivers which rush down from the Richthofen Range transforms the otherwise arid plain into one of great beauty and variety. The sandy expanse is intersected by irrigated belts of great fertility.

In certain localities there is a vast underground supply of good water which makes its way to the surface in countless springs. Where this happens the land produces wheat, rice, cotton, and an abundance of leguminous crops. Wide tracts are covered by fruit orchards, filled with apple, pear and apricot trees, by melon fields and vineyards. The life-giving rivers continue their course until they meet the all-devouring sands of Mongolia.

Between these large oases are strips of unirrigated land which sometimes take the form of loose sand, and sometimes of a springy alkaline deposit more hopelessly arid than the sand itself. The rivers are wide and shallow ; throughout the summer they are dangerous to cross, owing to sudden spates due to the rapid melting of the snows.

Along the northern margin of Kansu stretches the Great Wall of China, which is here far less impressive than it is in the Chihli Province. Still further north, however, the long line of earthworks is abruptly broken by the splendid brick fortress of Kia-yü-Kwan (Barrier of the Pleasant Valley). This is the Western Gate of China, twenty miles beyond the important city of Suchow. The inscriptions which surround this famous gate express in poignant terms the sadness and misgivings felt by the many thousands of Chinese settlers who pass through it into the distant regions beyond. One of the inscriptions has become so familiar that it is almost a proverb :

> " Forth from Kia-yü-Kwan,
> Eyes blinded with tears,
> Looking ahead, nothing but desert ;
> Looking behind, the Great Gate closed.
> Wife and Mother far from sight :
> Thinking upon them, tears will not cease."

At this point the Great Wall turns southwards, sealing the narrow opening between a stony ridge of low Mongolian hills and the impressive heights of the outer range of the Tibetan Alps.

The country beyond the Great Wall is known as *Kou wai* (Outside the Mouth). It is here that the Gobi Desert begins, although for a further space of eight marches oases are fairly frequent. Some of these are large and fertile ; from a distance they look like islands of green in an ocean of grit.

For centuries the Chinese Government has sent disgraced officials and criminals of a certain type to *Kou wai*. It has been the place of banishment, the country of exile. At certain periods, too, either by stratagem or by force, masses of people have been induced to migrate to *Kou wai*, in order to cultivate the waste land, and thus make a contribution to the Empire. Sometimes flood and famine in other parts of China have forced large groups of people to leave their homes and settle in this remote region.

The chief towns of *Kou wai* are Yümen, Tunghwang and Anhsi. The oasis of Tunghwang is famous for its temples, known as *The Caves of the Thousand Buddhas* and *The Lake of the Crescent Moon*. It is not easy to reach this town, for between it and the nearest oasis lies a stretch of desert which takes four days to cross, and the only water supply is bitter. The inhabitants of Tunghwang are exclusive, deeply conscious of their own historic importance, and proud to be citizens of a town which is known locally as Little Peking.

Anhsi is an ancient historic garrison outpost which served to guard the extreme border of China's protectorate against Tibetans, Uigurs, and other ancient enemies. At the present time it is being rapidly overtaken by the encircling sands which threaten it with the same fate as that which has overtaken so many of the buried cities of the Gobi Desert.

II.

The population presents features of great ethnological interest. Sinkiang, which lies to the north-west of Kansu, is China's most progressive colony, and attracts the more venturesome youths from all the eighteen provinces. Many of these emigrants never get beyond the Great Wall; this fact explains their presence in the towns of Kansu; in Kanchow and Suchow, for instance, the smithies' hammers are handled by Honan men, delicate china is most skilfully rivetted by the Szechwanese, and Shansi dialects greet the traveller from behind the money-changer's counter or in the pawnbroker's citadel. Few of the colonists give themselves to farming, and agriculture is almost entirely in the hands of the native peasants.

The native of the north-west belongs to a mixed race. His ancestry includes the remnants of Uigur, Yueh Chi and Tibetan tribes, in addition to the aboriginals who still exist as a class by themselves. The farmers are poor and illiterate, but through their ancestry (in particular the racial strain which they have inherited from the Uigur), they reveal occasionally an unexpected appreciation of the beauties of nature and art, which is not found among the more prosperous colonists. This is not surprising when we remember that during the eighth and ninth centuries the Uigurs attained a high level of artistic and literary culture.

Red and fair hair, blue or brown eyes and a ruddy complexion are not uncommon among these people. Much has been written of the signs of early civilization which have been discovered at Tunghwang, Kanchow and other places, and many a secluded village in North-West Kansu possesses a temple whose frescoes are worthy to be classed with the better-known art treasures exhibited in Western museums ; many of the monuments and temple decorations are so strongly reminiscent of the art of bygone civilizations, that by their means the path of ancient cultures can be traced.

III.

The missionary situation in North-West Kansu is unique. Before missionary societies were able to occupy the territory, a Chinese Christian man established himself in one of the largest towns of the district, and began aggressive missionary work.

In the year 1919, Dr. Kao, who had been employed in the Borden Hospital at Lanchow, took a medico-evangelistic journey through the north-west region of the Province. In the course of his travels he entered the town of Kanchow. His spirit was stirred within him as he beheld the city full of idols, and he reasoned in the market place daily with those whom he met. The populace said : " He seems to be a setter forth of strange gods," because he preached unto them " Jesus and the Resurrection."

Meanwhile, the young man became convinced that Kanchow was the place of God's appointment for him. In spite of a good deal of opposition, he was finally allowed to buy a piece of land, upon which he built a house and carried on his medical work. By this means he supported his wife and family.

After a few years, as a result of his efforts, a Christian community came into being, and the Indigenous Church manifested its zeal by a persistent attempt to reach the people of the surrounding towns and villages. Some of its members even sought to cross the borders of Kansu and enter Chinese Turkistan ; in the end, however, the material resources at their disposal proved insufficient for such an extensive undertaking, and they were forced to give up the idea. But, although the full plan could not be carried out, these men accomplished a great deal.

Work was further extended when three British women, members of the China Inland Mission, at the definite request of this Church, opened a Bible School in Suchow, where thirty Chinese Christian men and women were enrolled as students. By means of a course which combined Bible study with practical evangelism, a preaching band was formed, which carried the message of Christ to a wide and hitherto unevangelized region.

The two cities of Suchow and Kanchow are situated a week's journey apart and form admirable bases for pioneer work. In particular, the town of Suchow, the first city of China proper, lies only twenty miles within the western boundary of the Great Wall. It is a halting place for caravans, whether travelling eastward or westward. One suburb is used by Mongolian camel drivers for stalling their beasts, and another is mainly given up to Muslim inns where Turki traders carry on their business. It is at Suchow that all arrangements are made by caravans for the desert journeys. Teams are overhauled and carts repaired, while travellers enjoy a few days' rest in comparative comfort, free from the exertions and fatigues of the road. These conditions combine to make Suchow a strategic point of great importance, and at evangelistic services a constantly changing audience is easily secured. Christian books find a ready market among the moving population, and are thus carried to far distant places.

Kanchow, on the other hand, is a larger town with a more settled population. It is the nearest city to one of the most important passes in the Tibetan Alps, and the Tibetan people use its markets for the bartering of skins and gold dust in exchange for grain, tea and sugar.

One of the main evangelistic openings of the great North-West is afforded by the local fairs and religious festivals of its numerous temples, which are attended by men and women of all the surrounding villages. Large crowds never fail to assemble, and no opposition has hitherto been offered to the preacher who is thus able to make the very best use of his opportunity.

By crossing sandy belts for distances varying from twenty to fifty miles, fertile areas can be reached, for wherever there is water colonies of agriculturists are found. These colonies are very isolated and the people welcome with great enthusiasm any visitor from without. Preaching tents are crowded for every service, and the distribution and sale of books is most encouraging.

It is of paramount importance that the independence shown by the Chinese Church in North-West Kansu should be respected by the missionary societies. Assistance given by the foreign missionary to this, as to other indigenous organizations, should be clearly defined, both as regards its scope and its time limit. No assistance given should be of such a nature as to diminish the sense of responsibility which the local Church has recognized. The whole of this region should be evangelized by the Chinese themselves; the local Church is fit and ready for this enterprise.

CHAPTER IV.

Mongolia

I.

EVER since the days when Marco Polo crossed the plains of Turkistan into distant Cathay, and the days when the Tartar hosts of Asia burst into Russia and threatened the life of Europe, the names of Mongol and Mongolia* have held a certain fascination for Western peoples. Yet, until the last few years, Mongolia was actually one of the least-known countries in the world. Of late, however, the expeditions organized by the American Museum of Natural History, and other associations for archaeological research, have done something to overcome the great difficulties of travel, and thus to open up the country.

The grassy plateau of Mongolia is of great scientific interest, not only as the original home of pre-historic and giant reptiles, like the huge rhinoceros-like titanotherium and the gigantic baluchitherium, but also because there lie beneath its all-devouring sands and flower-strewn steppes the ruined cities and burying places of once populous and powerful kingdoms.

Mongolia lies immediately north of the Great Wall of China, and Chinese Turkistan; thus it separates both Sinkiang and China proper from Russia. The country is surrounded by mountains, and is a wide, shallow, basin-like plateau, lying at an altitude of three thousand to five thousand feet above sea level.

Broadly speaking, Mongolia may be divided into three parts: the North-Western region, which covers the high terrace of the plateau; the Gobi (using this

---

* The term " Mongolia," as it is found on modern maps, is used to describe the great northern province of China, whose boundaries have never been fixed with scientific precision. The term " Mongolia " to-day does not correspond with the Mongolia of earlier days, nor with the region of the same name ruled by the Mongol princes.

term in a wide sense), which occupies the lower terrace of the plateau, and South-Eastern Mongolia, which covers the eastern slope of the Khingan Mountains.

In North-Western Mongolia there are great tracts of forest and undulating steppes, where the flocks and herds of the semi-nomadic Mongols find pasture, and herds of antelopes and wild asses roam at will.

The glens of the Altai Mountains are a refreshing change from the plains. In springtime there is about them a freshness and fragrance which recalls the Scottish Highlands. The streams are full of water, and the sides of the valleys are clothed with larch and poplar, birch and willow. Sometimes a forest of larch will spread from the hills to the plain, joining the grassy meadows which are deep in flowers : gentian, purple and blue, crimson cyclamen, anemones, and masses of purple, violet, cream and yellow violas. These pastures are full of flocks, and here and there on the grassy hillside stand Kirei encampments. The whole of this region is well watered, and it contains several lakes. One of the largest of these lakes, named Kossogol, lies at an altitude of 5,320 feet above sea level, close to the Russian frontier, at the foot of a great snow mountain.

A great part of Mongolia is, however, very desolate. One-fourth of the country is either entirely desert, or, if it is not actually desert, it is so arid that only the poorest nomads can exist in it.

The great Gobi Desert is the deeper part of the enormous depression which fills the lower terrace of the vast Mongolian plateau. It looks like the dried-up bed of some huge primeval sea, and covers an area of over two hundred thousand square miles. This great expanse presents a varying appearance : in some parts it is crossed by ranges of hills, barren and empty of all signs of life ; in others it is an undulating plain, strewn with gravel, and dotted with mounds of clay ; in the district north of the Alashan Mountains there is nothing to be seen for hundreds of miles but bare sands, so wide, waterless, and unbroken that the Mongols call them *Tyngheri :* " the sky."

Throughout Mongolia and Dzungaria there are very few oases. The country suffers, in fact, from the lack of mountain ranges, with large glaciers and great snow fields to act as the source of streams in the desert. The consequence is that although sufficient grass is produced to support flocks throughout the year, they are obliged to wander from place to place in order to find the best pasture available.

We have here the obvious explanation of the nomadic life which is characteristic of these vast regions.

The prevailing impression left on the traveller's mind by this desert country is one of monotony and desolation, yet there are times when the sense of space is most exhilarating.

II.

The early centuries of Mongolian history are lost in a mist of legend. The founder of the first Mongol Empire was the redoubtable Genghiz Khan,* one of the greatest conquerors the world has ever known. From being merely the chief of a petty Mongolian tribe, he rose to be the ruler of an empire which extended from the China Sea to the banks of the Dnieper. Foremost among his descendants was Kublai Khan,† who became Emperor of China in A.D. 1280. Kublai was the first of his race to rise above the natural barbarism of the Mongols, yet he possessed a full measure of their virility and vigour. Through the story of Marco Polo the fame of this Mongol Emperor reached Europe. No great king arose after Kublai, and the reign of his ninth successor, Toghon Timur, ended in disgrace in 1368. The Mongols were expelled from China, and the rulers of the Ming Dynasty reigned in their stead.

The disintegration of the Empire of Genghiz Khan

---

* 1162–1227 A.D.   † 1216–1294 A.D.

and the fall of his dynasty in China were due to the Mongol incapacity to establish a settled form of government, or to gain the confidence and allegiance of conquered peoples.

Driven northwards and harried by the conquering Chinese, the Mongol tribes gradually broke away from all centralized government, and settled in scattered communities under their own chieftains throughout the vast region which lies between eastern Russia and Manchuria. In time some of these tribes were absorbed by Russia, and others by Turkey. Those who remained independent made their home in Eastern Mongolia.

After some years had elapsed the Mongols began to recover from the shock of the disaster which had befallen their race. Now and again they made successful raids into Tibet, and even into China. As the Chinese control over the frontier tribes weakened, the Mongols moved gradually southwards, and some of them even settled within the northern bend of the Yellow River. Thus it came about that when the Manchus overthrew the Ming Dynasty in 1644 the Mongol tribes were involved in the fortunes of China.

For nearly three hundred years Mongolia was a dependency of the Chinese Empire, and in 1911 she became an unwilling partner in the Chinese Republic.

III.

At the present day, for purposes of government, the Chinese divide Mongolia into two unequal portions : *Inner Mongolia*, the smaller, which lies to the south and east of the Gobi, and extends to the borders of China and Manchuria, and *Outer Mongolia*, which forms the rest of the country.

Inner Mongolia is divided into four districts, Jehol, Chahar, Sui Yuan and Sitao, containing much rich grass-growing prairie land and well-watered hill country. The Jehol territory alone claims more than half the total population of Mongolia.

Since the establishment of the Chinese Republic

there have been more changes in the political status of Mongolia than several previous centuries had witnessed.

After the fall of the Manchus, in 1911, the Mongol princes expelled the Chinese officials from Urga, declared the independence of Outer Mongolia and proclaimed the Bogdo Lama, or Huktuktu, as ruler, under the title of Bogdo Khan. Russia immediately stepped in to recognize and " protect " this new state. Despite a belated and ineffective " cancellation of autonomy " in 1920, by means of a petition to Peking signed by representatives of the Chinese residents and Mongolian Council of Ministers in Urga, there is to-day a Soviet Government established in Urga, the capital, in direct communication and collaboration with Moscow. Some of the young Mongol leaders have been educated in Moscow, and their attitude towards religion is largely that of the Soviet leaders in Russia.

Of late years the Mongols have become increasingly awake to the hopelessness of their condition : to their need of education and of political, social and religious reform. Recent events in China, Russia, and the world at large, have so shaken their self-complacency that at least in Outer Mongolia they have received with some show of willingness the proffered help of Soviet Russia. In common with other Far Eastern nations, Mongolia was represented by delegates at a " Conference of the Toilers of the Far East," held in Moscow, in January, 1922, under the auspices of the Communist International.

On the 20th of May, 1924, the Huktuktu—Living Buddha, Pope of Mongol Buddhism and ruler of the country—died in Urga, and the Soviet authorities immediately announced that no one was to be elected in his place. Further, it was decreed that all lamas under forty years of age were to return to civil, and presumably to family, life ; in future, also, no more acolytes were to be trained. Thus the power of the corrupt system of Lamaism seems to have been broken, even though it may continue to linger for a while. " Here the Soviets have struck shrewder blows at

Buddhism—the dead hand on Mongolian manhood for four hundred years—than they have in Russia at Byzantine Christianity. And the awakening and fertilization of Mongolian youth which will follow the break-up of monastic life may well bear a big surprise in the coming generation."*

The feudal princes, who held the right of life and death over their " property," have been largely deprived of power. All class distinctions, and titles like " prince," " official," " noble," and " saint," have been abrogated, and their holders are disqualified both from electing and from being elected to office.

Further, on the 31st of May, 1924, a Sino-Soviet Treaty was signed recognizing that " Outer Mongolia is an integral part of the Republic of China and respecting China's sovereignty therein " ; at the same time it is stated that Mongolia enjoys an " autonomy so far-reaching as to preclude Chinese interference with internal affairs," and that " Mongolia has settled down and been consolidated on a basis somewhat similar to the Soviet System."† In November of the same year the first assembly of the new Mongol Parliament (the Huruldan or People's Assembly) was convoked. In the text of its Constitution it proclaimed that Outer Mongolia is an independent republic without a president, and that the Seal and Supreme Power of the Bogdo Khan (Holy Ruler) has been transferred to the People's Assembly.

Moreover, in the " Declaration of Rights of the Labouring (*sic*) People of Mongolia " " the fundamental principle is laid down as a guarantee of the religious liberty of the labouring masses," that the Church is separate from the State, and that " Religion is the private concern of every citizen."

Although Outer Mongolia is largely cut off from other parts of the world, the young Republic spares no effort to maintain the closest relations with Moscow

---

* W. E. D. Allen. *The Times*, 24th June, 1929.

† Georgiy Chicherin, People's Commissary for Foreign Affairs since 1918.

and the U.S.S.R. The Soviet-Mongol Railway Agreement of 1926 seeks to link up Mongolia by rail with the Trans-Siberian route, by steamship on the Selenga and Orkhon Rivers, by the telegraph system, and, eventually by regular airship services connecting Urga with Werkne-Udinsk and Chita. Towards the south a railway has been projected linking up Urga and Kalgan, and at present a regular motor service operates for passenger traffic between these places. Merchandise is still carried by camel caravans. The real cultural, political and economic connections are with the north ; and there is no indication that there is any relationship between the Nanking Government and that of Urga.

Most effective of all the Soviet methods, however, is that of indirect propaganda. The Russian film, *Storm over Asia*, which has been described as " an artistic masterpiece," cannot fail to make a strong appeal to the awakening minds of Mongolian youth. This film is the story of a Mongol shepherd boy, who is robbed by Buddhist bonzes, swindled by American fur-dealers, and ill-treated by White Russian soldiers. Suddenly the " White " general discovers that the lad is a descendant of Genghiz Khan and he sets him up as a puppet prince in Urga. Finally the young Mongol " prince " rouses the people, and in a lightning cavalry charge the Mongol horsemen sweep away the White troops. That is the story. " The appeal is double-barrelled—to the community of sympathy of the Russian and Asiatic workers, and, more subtly, to the traditional military ' superiority-complex ' of the Central Asian peasants "*—the descendants of Genghiz Khan.

IV.

In appearance the Mongol is dirty and unkempt. His unwashed face and hands are scarcely surprising in a land of biting winds, cruel frosts, and little water,

---

* *The Times*, 24th June, 1929.

where the traveller often has to decide whether he will drink the precious liquid or wash in it. His hair is tousled, and his shaggy, greasy sheep-skin garments may raise a prejudice against him. If to his unattractive appearance and primitive habits are added fatalism, lack of ambition, laziness, love of strong drink, quick temper, and a religiously perverted sense of right and wrong, the worst has been said of the average Mongol, for, although he is held in bondage by a religion paralysing in its grip and fatal to any growth in personal character, the Mongol yet retains much natural attractiveness.

He is simple-minded, fearless and self-reliant, generous and comparatively honest, kindly and hospitable, and, when he is understood and treated with proper consideration, he is quite approachable, although he is sensitive and quick to resent slights. He is capable, willing and trustworthy. Inured to a life of hardship, he seldom grumbles, and is patient and cheerful under difficulties. In business he is no match for the subtle Chinese, whom he distrusts, but in simple-hearted manliness and in all martial pursuits the Mongol is more than his equal.

Across Mongolia's vast territory its people, who are grouped in a Feudal Federation, live their simple pastoral lives, dwelling in tents and huts on the grassy plains, moving their encampments according to season, water supply and condition of the pastures, much as their ancestors have done for centuries.

The divisions of the people are as follows :—

Princes and officials of the old hereditary nobility of varying ranks, or free people ; taxpayers, or serfs ; lamas, or celibate monks of varying hierarchal rank, or "lords spiritual" ; and their vassals, or serfs.

The local administrative unit is the Hosho, the " banner " or tribe, forming the fief of any one ruling prince, who controls his people through civil officers and military vassals ; the latter provide their quota of mounted warriors when required and administer a modern adaptation of the Code of Genghiz Khan.

The eighty-six Hosho, or Tribes, of Outer Mongolia are grouped into four Aimaks or Khanates, being groups of one or more Principalities (Hosho) forming the feudal inheritance of one princely family bound together by ties of direct descent and heredity ; the senior living prince of the reigning family is considered the head of the Aimak. These rulers are called the Tsetsen, Tushetu, Sainnoin and Tsasaktu Khans.

The fifty-seven Principalities, or tribes, of Inner Mongolia are confederated into six Leagues (Chinese " Meng "), not identical with the Aimak, but designed by the Manchus to weaken the tribal organization. A senior prince is elected by his peers in the associated tribes, but confirmed in office by the Chinese Government. These are the names of the six Leagues : the Djerim, Djosotu, Djouda, Silingol, Ulan-tsab and Iehedzu.*

V.

The religion of Mongolia is Lamaism. Introduced into Tibet from India in the seventh century before Christ, it was accommodated to Tibetan superstition and demonology, but it was not imposed upon the Mongols until the reign of Kublai Khan.

---

* To complete the summary we ought to mention the various scattered groups of Mongols living mainly outside Mongolia, not including the Buriat Mongols of the Baikal regions of Siberia.
1. Alashan Oleuts—west of the Yellow River.
2. Elsin-gol Turguts—of Central Asia.
3. Kokonor and Tsaidam Mongols—twenty-nine tribes.
4. Ili and Tarbagatai Mongols—of Dzungaria, some seventeen tribes.
5. Altai Mongols—of Kobdo and Sinkiang, some ten tribes.
6. Darhat, or tribes of Turkis—in North-West Mongolia, now forming a small " independent " Tannu-Tubin (Soviet) Republic.
7. Mannai Oleut Mongols—in North Manchuria west of Tsitsihar.
8. Mongol Bannermen—in and around Peking and Jehol, where with the Manchus they formerly performed garrison duties.
9. Shabunars or serfs of the late Bogdo Lama of Urga, some two hundred thousand in number, have since his death and the abolition of his office as spiritual and temporal head of the country, been formed into eight Hosho under special Jassaks (princes).

Gradually an elaborate temple service was built up, which is still in daily use. Twice a day at least in the lamaseries portions of the sacred Tibetan scriptures are chanted in deep-toned voices by robed and mitred monks, sitting cross-legged in rows before the image of Buddha, presided over by an enthroned " living Buddha," or abbot. These chants are accompanied by the sound of drums, bells, conch-shells, cymbals and enormous trumpets, twenty feet long, with the sprinkling of holy water, and the burning of incense.

The more ethical and spiritual teaching of original Buddhism has been replaced by a system of magic spells and meaningless ritual, the external observance of which is held to be the full equivalent of the practice of all the virtues. The mere repetition of these ritual acts has power to coerce the spirits and to bring deliverance and happiness to those who pray. Hence the never-ending repetition of the cryptic words, practically the only prayer of the Tibetan and the Mongol : " Om mane padme hum " (O, thou jewel in the lotus flower !). This pathetic invocation and other equally meaningless prayers enclosed in cylinders are piously set in motion by means of windmills and prayer wheels, or inscribed on flags that flutter from the tops of dwellings, trees and sacred piles of stones. The mystic syllables are often carved on the rocks or in huge characters on the hillside. Told by the fingers on the never-absent rosary, muttered with the lips in the crowded market or when crossing the lonely plain ; morning, noon and night, at birth and in death, and on every occasion, the same futile cry for deliverance continues to ascend to heaven from a race held fast in the bondage of sin.

The effect of this religion upon the Mongol has been extraordinary. On the one hand, it has done much " to restrain the Mongols' predatory and savage instincts, quenching in them the thirst for blood, and implanting certain religious ideas and ideals, however inadequate. Yet, on the other hand, it has robbed their manhood of its energy and natural ambition,

seared and beclouded their conscience as to moral
guilt, and strangled all progress, intellectual activity
and moral endeavour. At the same time, through its
tyrannous, depraved and corrupting priesthood—the
lamas composing more than sixty per cent. of the
male population and universally characterized by
unblushing and unnatural wickedness—it has not only
degraded worship and prayer to a mechanical ritual
but it has debased womanhood, destroyed the sanctity
of family life, flooded the land with immorality, and
made its religious establishments hot-beds of vice.''

As a result of this drain upon the nation's vital
strength the population has steadily declined, and the
only hope of preserving the Mongols from ultimate
extinction lies in their deliverance from the power
and blight of Lamaism into the glorious liberty of the
children of God.

VI.

About one hundred years ago the pioneer
missionaries, Swan, Stallybrass and Yuille, of the
London Missionary Society, settled among the Buryat
Mongols on the Siberian frontier. There, on the banks
of the Selenga River and its neighbourhood, they
laboured for over twenty years, until the work was
stopped by order of the Tsarist Government. The
whole Bible was translated into classical Mongolian,
and ever since it has been of the utmost value to those
who have endeavoured to evangelize the Mongol
race.

About thirty years later, in 1885, the devoted
James Gilmour (also of the London Missionary Society)
began his itinerations. He felt that the work among
the nomads was not very promising, and thought that
his time might be more profitably spent among the
settled Mongols and Chinese in the south-eastern
parts of Mongolia. For this reason he made his headquarters at Chao Yang, where he gathered a few
splendid converts from the Chinese. He was joined

by John Parker, of the London Missionary Society, who carried on the work after Gilmour died in 1891. In 1897, Dr. Thomas Cochrane joined Mr. Parker and started medical mission work. By the year 1900, at three or four centres, groups of Chinese Christians had been gathered into small churches.

After the Boxer Rising, when all missionary effort in Inner Mongolia was brought to a standstill, this work was handed over to the Irish Presbyterian Mission, who in their turn transferred it to the Brethren missionaries in 1912. At that time the Church at Chao Yang was composed solely of Chinese members. Since then the Brethren missionaries have carried on a work characterized by steady growth. Dr. Case, one of their number, died at Chao Yang, and has recently been succeeded by Dr. Soutter, who has revived the hospital work. Dispensary work is carried on at four of their stations. Primary schools for boys and girls are distinctive of their work everywhere. These missionaries are particularly active in Bible distribution, in connection with which they undertake extended itinerations. Periodical Bible schools are also held. Every station records converts ; at Chao Yang, the oldest of the former London Missionary Society stations, there is a membership of one hundred and forty.

Of all the missions now at work in Inner Mongolia, that carried on by the Brethren, which was begun at Pa Kow in 1887, is the oldest. Since then seven new missions have entered the country.

The *Scandinavian Alliance Mission* has established an agricultural and industrial colony as an experiment at Patsebolong on a large tract of land just north of the Ordos Desert, irrigated from the Yellow River. A new station has recently been opened at Wangtefu. This Mission has about four workers.

The *Swedish Mongol Mission* began work in 1899 at Halong-Osso, eighty miles north of Kalgan, and since then has extended its work to Gulchagan, Hattin-Sum and Doyen. Owing to changes in the migration of the Chinese, the work at Halong-Osso has been given up. Including those on furlough, this Mission has now eleven workers. It has also one hospital and one dispensary, with two doctors and two nurses.

The *Assemblies of God Mission* has established several stations in Chahar, with nine or ten workers.

The *Swedish Alliance Mission* works in association with the China Inland Mission, and its field of operations is in Sui Yuan and Chahar. The work is steadily growing and is organized into eight churches, and missionaries live at eight centres. There are ten out-stations. In the Sunday schools there are about five hundred children. Day schools number seven and are attended by equal numbers of boys and girls. At present the Bible school is closed. In the industrial school there are fifty-eight students, and in the two children's homes about three hundred children. There are three dispensaries which treated two hundred patients last year, and one hospital which dealt with fifty-nine patients. The Mission has one European nurse and three Chinese nurses, but no doctor. Although the majority of the inhabitants of this region are Chinese, most of the land is owned by the Mongol princes, to whom taxes are paid.

The *Hephzibah Faith Mission* opened work in 1922 at Chininghsien in Chahar, where it now has four missionaries.

In 1923, the *Kremmer Mennonite Brethren Church* began work at Chotzeshan in Chahar; it has a staff of six workers.

The *Brethren Mission*, which has already been mentioned, carries on work in the Jehol territory of Eastern Inner Mongolia, among the Chinese and the tribes of the Djosotu and Djouda Leagues. It has five stations and thirty-two missionaries.

The *Salvation Army* has been extending its work since 1918, and has missionaries at two or three stations. It has opened work at Fengchen, the capital of Chahar.

In addition to these missions located in Mongolia, the *Irish Presbyterian Mission* and the *Danish Mission* carry on Mongol work from two or three stations in Manchuria.

The *British and Foreign Bible Society* serves all the missions. From its headquarters at Kalgan it touches not only Inner Mongolia, but also the northern Marches of the Chinese provinces, Chihli and Shansi.

Although the region which lies beyond the Gobi Desert is still closed to Christian missions, Bible Society agents make tours in this district as opportunity offers. Until the present time these journeys have been tedious and hard, mostly by camel. The motor-car service recently established between Urga and Kalgan provides new facilities for Bible distribution. Even working on the older and slower lines, the British and Foreign Bible Society colporteurs sold over one hundred and seventy-six thousand books (mostly portions in *Mongolian*) in 1928. These figures vary from year to year ; in 1927 they were nearly one hundred thousand more than in 1928. In all the mission hospitals, every patient hears the Word and leaves with a Gospel in his bundle. Mongolian Scriptures are still in demand even as far west as Sinkiang. The Bible Society has published Scriptures in four forms of *Mongolian :* (1) *Literary or Classical Mongolian,* in which the whole Bible is available, translated in the middle of last century by the London Missionary Society missionaries, Stallybrass, Swan and Yuille, assisted by learned Buryats, most of whom were lamas. Their version of the Gospels was afterwards revised by two Bible Society agents and a Mongol from Urga, named Serim Pon Sok ; (2) *Buryat or Northern Mongolian,* spoken principally round Lake Baikal, has St. Matthew's Gospel with the Russian version alongside ; (3) *Kalmuk or Western Mongolian* is spoken by nomads on the eastern part of the Tien Shan Range, on the western border of the Gobi Desert, and even as far west as the Kalmuk Steppes in South-East Russia. The complete New Testament has been issued in this dialect ; (4) *Khalka or Eastern Mongolian,* is used from the Great Wall of China to the River Amur and right across the Gobi Desert as far as the Altai Mountains.

St. Matthew's Gospel, prepared by a Mongol lama and revised by foreign missionaries, was first published in 1872, and another edition was issued in 1894.

From Manchuria, at the north-east corner of this unoccupied field, over four hundred thousand copies of Scripture were sold in 1928, some of which no doubt found their way far west across the Khingan Mountains. The *Manchu* version of the New Testament will always be associated with the name of George Borrow, who saw an edition through the press at St. Petersburg almost a hundred years ago. This Manchu New Testament, first published in 1835, has just (1929) been reproduced by photography in Shanghai to meet the present needs.

On the eastern side, Central Asia is bounded by China, and from that quarter Scriptures in the various forms of *Chinese* are frequently being sent to many far distant places from the Depôt in Shanghai. Even during the upheavals of the last few years, in spite of difficulties of transport, dangers to colporteurs (more than one has lost his life in carrying out his arduous task) and the disorganization of large parts of the country, the circulation of Scriptures from the British and Foreign Bible Society Agency (and this includes Central Asia) has been greater than ever. The latest figures reach the marvellous total of 3,951,809. The reports of the colporteurs speak of the wonderful and pathetic willingness on the part of the people to spare coppers from their scanty means to buy copies of the Gospels.

In *Outer Mongolia* for a time the *Swedish Mongol Mission* occupied the town of Urga, until it was expelled by the Soviet authorities. Thus there is now no mission in Outer Mongolia.

Although *Inner Mongolia* has remained open for mission work, the conditions among the Mongols are such that it is one of the hardest fields in Eastern Asia. A few heroic missionaries have remained at their posts through the recent months of war and famine. The apparent results of their labours are small. It is reported that three Mongolians were baptized last year (1928).

The work of these eight Societies is still largely among the growing Chinese population and those Mongols who can be reached. Among the small number of Mongol Christians, some show such sterling Christian character that the future is not without promise. The Christian witness of Europeans, Chinese and Mongols, should have a greater and greater effect. James Gilmour said : " I am still of opinion that our best way to reach the Mongols is from a Chinese base." Of late years this possibility has been placed in the hands of the Church. A marked feature of the present situation in Mongolia is the steady flow of Chinese immigration from Shantung. This process of infiltration is for the first time in history setting the plough to the fertile valleys and well-watered prairies of Southern Mongolia, a country which bids fair to compare with Siberia and Canada as one of the great granaries of the world. This fact presents an unparalleled opportunity for the evangelization of Mongolia.

On a recent evangelistic journey a missionary discovered three new Chinese districts in course of being marked out on the best grasslands of the Djouda League. They are veritable islands of Chinese culture in the midst of the simple pastoral life of the plains and valleys on the south-eastern slopes of the great Khingan range. The same thing is happening from the Manchurian side among the tribes of the Djerim League. One of Marshal Feng's constructive efforts has been to encourage this emigration of Chinese families to similar regions outside the Great Wall north of the Shansi and Shensi provinces.

The burden of the evangelization of the surrounding Mongols must, therefore, be laid mainly on the Chinese Christians. Theirs is a very special responsibility, even greater than that of the foreign missionary. It may be said that the Chinese have not proved acceptable evangelists to the Mongols, on account of the friction arising from land settlements and trade relationships. But the Chinese Christians will have to face this difficulty which is no greater and perhaps not so great as that of the European or any other

foreigner.   One of the most acceptable evangelists
among the Mongols was Liu Yi, a Chinese who helped
Gilmour.   He spoke Mongol fluently and was on most
friendly terms with the people.

The centres of light are still few, and the darkness
is very dense. " Mongolia to us seems a great spiritual
wilderness. Generations have come and gone without
knowing God : still they come and go. Perhaps there
is something in the hard climatic conditions of the
country which has withered the souls of the people
or hardened their hearts. The long, long winter ; the
wild winds which sweep across the desert ; the hard
hoarless frost which for months checks all vegetable
life ; the sudden and short-lived spring with the
scanty rains it brings, followed by parching heat and
storms of dust in summer ; these conditions seem to
have repressed the finer human elements in Mongol
character."*

The Mongols are scattered over an immense area,
and their nomadic habits make all efforts to approach
them with the Gospel very difficult. Only men of strong
physique and great powers of endurance can stand the
hardships of life in this land. But difficulties of this
kind have never deterred the heralds of the Cross.
The societies which are at present working in Mongolia,
however, need a larger measure of support. With a
view to effective work in the future, there is need for
some definite co-ordination of policy among the
missions. Plans for reaching the Mongols of the remoter
regions should be formed on an intelligent basis of
co-operation, in order to avoid the mistakes which
have often hampered missionary work in the past.

Work among people of such nomadic habits must
necessarily be of a simple nature, whether it be
evangelistic, educational or medical. It is of supreme
importance to teach converts from the beginning the
New Testament ideal of the Church. Wherever two
or three meet in fellowship, there the Church with all
its privileges and responsibilities exists.   This living

---

* *The Bible in China.* Report for 1928, page 28.

fellowship possesses all the resources of Christ's Body, and should from the first be encouraged to exercise its spiritual functions. The hope of the future lies not with scattered converts, but in such small living groups. They are living branches of Christ's Church, no matter how few and poor their members. In all difficult fields like Mongolia, this supreme spiritual conception of the Church and its divine prerogatives should be kept in view all the time. From such living units, even when only the " Church in the house of Feng," the Church of Christ will grow. Thus, from the beginning the definite aim should be : a self-supporting Church, full of evangelistic fervour, sending forth its witnesses to the furthest limits of Mongolia.

CHAPTER V.

Tibet

I.

"ALL roads lead to Rome," and in Tibet "All roads lead to Lhasa." But along whatever road the traveller comes, from India or from China, always he must cross a high mountain barrier. On every side the country is enclosed within long ranges of snow-capped mountains : on the south by the Himalayas and the transverse ranges of Upper Yunnan, on the east by the western mountainous borderland of Yunnan, Szechwan and Kansu, on the north by the Kuen Lun Range, and on the west, where it narrows to a breadth of only one hundred and fifty miles, by the junction of the Karakoram Mountains with the Himalayas. It is not difficult to see why Tibet has gained the title of the Great Closed Land. From the point of view of geography it is more difficult to approach than almost any other country in the world. Further, its great altitude* is a strain on all foreigners who have been used to living at ordinary levels, and the journeys over the mountain passes are fatiguing, difficult and often dangerous. It is significant that no great armies have ever passed through Tibet to invade India ; even Genghiz Khan led his troops round through Bukhara and Afghanistan in order to avoid the necessity of crossing Tibet by the direct route.

The most well-known highway into Tibet passes through Sikkim. The road crosses the frontier near

---

* Tibet is the highest country in the world : the tablelands have an average height of nearly 17,000 feet ; the mountain peaks rise to a height varying from 20,000 to 24,000 feet, and the passes range from 16,000 to 19,000 feet above the sea. Several of the great rivers of Asia—the Indus, Brahmaputra, Irrawaddy, Mekong and Yangtze—rise in this mountain region, and flow down into the valleys and plains of India, Siam, Yunnan and Szechwan.

Pharijong, a little town through which passes all the trade of southern Tibet with India. Pharijong is one of the highest places in the world inhabited by man, and is one of the dirtiest. The name means literally " Hill of the Pig," and nothing could be more apt.* Yet as the traveller gains the summit of the pass, and looks down on the town, it is not the filthy little frontier station that grips his attention, but the view. The valleys behind him may be filled with mist, but ahead it seems as though all Tibet lay spread out before him. It is a marvellous expanse of mountain country, range upon range of brown, bare hills, all clear-cut and distinct, while behind them towers one pure white peak, Chomolhari—" divine mother of mountains "—serene and ineffable, against a cloudless sky of turquoise blue.

Beyond Pharijong the road winds up and down, now through desolate valleys, cold and windswept, then over snow-covered passes out on to the high tableland, with its boggy soil broken up by tussocks of grass and numerous lakes and tarns. In summer the same track will wear a different aspect : the valleys and the lower slopes of the barren hills will be clothed with fresh green grass and flowers. Blue larkspurs, orange marigolds and familiar yellow dandelions stand out among a mass of less familiar blossoms, purple and pink and white. Tiny ferns cling to every crevice in the rock, vetches and violet primulas spring from the very face of the rock itself, while the dark blue spires of monkshood mingle with all this beauty " like devils in heaven."† All along the route the vivid sky-blue Tibetan poppy is easily the most striking flower in the country, while on the high tableland the dark gorges and level river valleys are often lit up by brilliant patches of yellow mustard blossom.

One of the most wonderful sights on the road to

---

* See *The Land of the Lama :* by David MacDonald, page 256.
† This is the *Aconitum Luridum ;* its roots contain a deadly poison.

Lhasa is the "Turquoise Lake," or Yam-Dok-Tso. Few foreigners have ever seen it, for it does not lie on the direct route to the capital. The waters are of an exquisite blue-green, ringed by clean shores of pure white sand. Solitary and still it lies among its enfolding hills. Here and there near the shore are little patches of cultivated ground, and wherever the springing barley pushes its way through the earth there also will be a sheet of forget-me-nots. On the margin of the Lake the ruins of ancient castles add the final touch of romance to the scene, while beyond, on the horizon, are the eternal glaciers of the Himalayas, a silver setting for the "Turquoise Lake."

II.

The first sight of Lhasa is as unexpected as it is beautiful. Standing on the height overlooking the city the traveller gazes with amazement at the stretches of green woodland, and marshy grass, watered by streamlets of clear brown water winding among the over-arching trees. The whole city is surrounded by this belt of luxuriant vegetation, a mile in depth. The town itself is overshadowed and completely dominated by the Potala, the great Palace-Temple of the Grand Lama. Its massive white stone walls rise from a sea of green. The central building stands out impressively between wide blocks of masonry of glowing crimson. It is crowned with glittering golden roofs, shining and dazzling against the pale blue sky. This Palace is a "marvel in stone," nine hundred feet long, and seventy feet higher than St. Paul's Cathedral. There is an utter disproportion between this great Palace-Temple of the Potala and the town which lies at its feet. It seems to symbolize the gulf that separates the people of Tibet from their priests.

After this striking approach the town itself seems almost insignificant. It consists of large groups of houses, separated by dark and narrow lanes. Here and there are squares or patches of waste ground.

The poorest quarter of the city is as dirty as Pharijong, and even more repulsive.   Yet in these loathsome surroundings the flowers bloom better than elsewhere : nasturtiums trail their gold and flame-coloured blossoms over the decaying walls ; tall bright hollyhocks spring from the oozing black mud, and crimson stocks, with their delicate grey-green leaves, strive to cover the filth of the dust-heaps upon which they grow.

Amid a tangle of dark and dirty lanes stands the great temple, the Jokang, built in A.D. 652. The outside of the building is unpromising, but the interior is one of the most interesting sights in Central Asia.   Its chief treasure is an image of the Buddha, golden and magnificent, lit up by the soft radiance of countless butter lamps. The face is that of Gautama as a young and eager prince, and the image is ornamented with masses of precious stones. This temple is the Holy of Holies for the whole of Northern Buddhism.

III.

"There is no approach to God unless a lama leads the way"—so runs the Tibetan proverb. The word *Lama* means literally "Superior One," and theoretically it should be applied only to the Abbots of monasteries ; in practice, however, it has come to be used of every member of the Tibetan priesthood.   It is estimated that the Lamas form one-sixth of the adult male population of Tibet. The term "Lamaism" is often applied to Tibetan religion, but it is not accurate. The religion of Tibet is Buddhism, derived from and identical with the Indian Buddhism of the *Mahayana*. The Tibetans themselves say that they are believers in "Buddha's religion" or "the orthodox religion."*

---

* The pre-Buddhist religion of Tibet was called the Bon religion. It is a necromantic cult with devil-dancing. Although strictly forbidden by the lamas of Central and Western Tibet, it is nevertheless largely and openly professed over the greater part of Eastern and South-Eastern Tibet, where Chinese influence is strong. It is particularly popular among the settled agricultural population.

It seems probable that Buddhism was introduced into Tibet in the seventh century of the Christian era, that is, about twelve hundred years after the death of the Buddha.

Buddhism in Tibet has developed the teaching and practice of its founder to great extremes. Since salvation is bound up with the monastic state, monasticism has here reached greater proportions than in any other country in the world. For centuries the government of the land has been in the hands of the monks themselves. At the head of the priesthood are the Dalai Lama and the Tashi Lama. In theory the Tashi Lama, whose headquarters are at Shigatse, is superior to the Dalai Lama, who lives at Lhasa. In practice, however, the Dalai Lama is supreme, since he alone wields secular as well as religious authority.

Thus there has arisen the strange phenomenon of a social order dominated by thousands of celibate monks, who lead a parasitic existence and decimate the people. Since Buddhism was introduced into the country, the Tibetans, who were at one time virile and enterprising, have steadily declined both in power and in numbers, until now the population has decreased to a tenth of its former size. In a land more than six times as large as Great Britain, there are only from two to three million people, who live in about 13,000 towns and villages. It is possible, however, to ride for many miles without seeing a trace of human life.

The country is dotted with monasteries, great and small. Most of them have been built in retired and beautiful spots. Some are perched high up among the mountains, in rocky fastnesses, where the buildings seem part of the rock itself ; others are built in sheltered valleys, or on low hills in the plains, where they have glorious views of the surrounding country. Near Lhasa there are three large lamaseries with a total population of over twenty thousand monks. Of these three Drepung is the largest monastery in the world ; it is situated about three and a half miles away from the western gate of Lhasa. The monks are more like

F

mercenary soldiers than anything else, and during popular festivals their armed regiments terrorize the people of the capital. Besides these large monasteries there are numbers of smaller ones inhabited by groups of lamas varying from four or five to one hundred. Some of these lamaseries are wealthy and prosperous, but others are simply collections of poor and squalid huts.

From the earliest days of Tibetan Buddhism there have always been some souls full of a passionate longing for spiritual enlightenment; impelled by this desire they have left the ordinary ways of men. Sometimes the period of solitude has been short; others have secluded themselves for twelve years; a few Lamas leave the world for ever. In the neighbourhood of Gyantse there is a hermitage where monks shut themselves up in dark stone huts for the rest of their lives. This hermitage was founded in the year 1100 by a great hermit saint, and ever since it has usually been inhabited. A hermit retires into his voluntary prison for a first period of three months and three days. He then comes out and goes through a special course of study and preparation for the next period of retirement, which is supposed to last for three years, three months and three days. During this second period many lamas begin to suffer in mind, and some of them entirely lose their reason. At the end of this period the hermit comes forth once more to prepare for the final term of imprisonment which will end only with his death.

The Lamas look down upon the laity, calling them " the dark ignorant people " and " the worldly ones," though sometimes they are kind enough to give them the title of " the givers of alms," making it quite clear, however, that it is the givers who gain most by this exercise of charity. The people accept the authority of the Lamas without question, and give lavishly towards their support.

The ordinary people are kindly, hard-working, cheerful, and hospitable; they are also extremely courteous and well-mannered. David MacDonald says that " on the roads everyone who passes by has a cheery word and a smile for one, even the very poor and the beggars protruding their tongues to the full extent as a sign of greeting. This tongue-protruding takes a little getting used to, before the traveller new to Tibet realizes it is all meant in respect, and not as rudeness." Their main occupations are agriculture, cattle and sheep raising, and trade. The two trade centres are Pharijong on the Indian trade route, and Chamdo on the Chinese frontier. The daily life is hard, for the climate is severe, and there is little comfort in the houses of the poorer people.

Religious ideas play a leading part in everyday life. The doctrine of Karma and of the transmigration of the soul, and the insistence upon the importance of acquiring merit by good deeds, affect the life of the laity in many ways. The spirit of Buddhism dominates their folk-lore, their proverbs, and their songs and plays. It influences their attitude towards animals, prohibiting any careless sacrifice of life. Crime is punished with ruthless severity, and mutilation is a common form of punishment.

The popular religion has, however, some very striking non-Buddhist features, derived from the Bon religion which preceded Buddhism. The hardness of life in such a severe climate, where the forces of nature seem like implacable enemies, leads the Tibetans to believe that their disasters are due to the activity of malignant spirits. Hence their craving for protection by means of charms and amulets which everyone wears, even the Lamas themselves. Pilgrimages are popular, and prayers are ever on the lips of the people. Day and night the prayer-flags flutter in the breeze, the people turn their prayer-wheels and use their rosaries ; yet with all their strivings they never enter into peace.

IV.

The rule of the Lamas dates from the time of Kublai Khan and of Gushi Khan, his Tartar successor

in Central Asia. Kublai Khan appointed the Abbot
of Sakya as ruler of Tibet ; Gushi Khan transferred
the control to the priests and created the office of
Dalai Lama ; this official together with the Tashi
Lama became the source of all the power in the State.
Gradually, however, the political power came to be
vested solely in the Dalai Lama, while the influence
of the Tashi Lama was limited to purely religious
functions and ceremonies.

In 1720 China drove out the Tartar overlords from
Tibet and thus secured a certain amount of control
over the country. Relations between China and Tibet,
however, remained uneasy and uncertain, and the
political question of the Sino-Tibetan border has never
been entirely settled. The political situation assumed
a new aspect in 1914 when Tibet signed a treaty with
India* which completely transformed its political
position. From being a reluctantly dependent country,
it became an independent autonomous State.

To-day Tibet stands at the parting of the ways.
Lhasa, the Sacred City, the conservative stronghold
of Lamaism, has been besieged in the seeming security
of its isolation, and that in the most subtle manner,
for the foe is no external one, but dwells within its own
walls.

The Younghusband Mission of 1904–05 may be
said to mark the beginning of modern history in Tibet,
and, since the visit of the Dalai Lama to India, Lhasa
has become the scene of the efforts of the progressive
party, which has outlined a tentative scheme of
reform.

At present the only roads in Tibet are those which
have been worn by the great caravans travelling to
and fro, but plans are in the air for better roads and
for the construction of a light railway. Reformers
have succeeded in establishing a regular postal service
between the chief towns, and in the installation of

---

* Simla Convention, 3rd July, 1914. For a full account of this political development, see *Europe and the East*, by N. D. Harris, chapter X.
Cf. also *The People of Tibet*, by Sir Charles Bell, chapter II.

telegraph and telephone lines from Darjeeling to Lhasa. It is not surprising that there is much opposition to such reforms in a land which has prided itself for centuries upon its rigid isolation. The progressive party, although comparatively small, is favoured by the Dalai Lama himself, and includes within its ranks some outstanding men.

The vast majority of the Lamas are opposed to all reform and to every kind of innovation, whether secular or religious. At the same time there are signs which suggest that the progressive element cannot be measured merely in terms of numbers.

Whatever changes the future may hold for Tibet, the modern movements which have recently taken place seem to have rendered the country more exclusive than ever. Strangely enough institutions like the post and the telegraph are proving the means of shutting the door against European intrusion.

A Tibetan proverb says : " The goal will not be reached if the right distance be not travelled," and when so much power is vested in the conservative, clerical party, whose influence over the people is unlimited, it is useless to expect that the whole situation can suddenly be transformed by a handful of " moderns." Until some degree of enlightenment can penetrate the ignorance and gross superstition of the lama hierarchy, there is little hope of either spiritual or material progress in Tibet.

V.

The first follower of Christ to penetrate into the mountain fastnesses of Tibet was *Friar Odoric of Pordenone*, who is said to have reached Lhasa by way of China about 1328. " Going on further," says Odoric, " I came to a certain Kingdom called Tibet. . . . The people of this country do for the most part live in tents made of black felt. Their principal city is surrounded with fair and beautiful walls . . . curiously put

together."*   Two hundred years passed before any
further attempt was made to enter the country in the
Name of Christ.   *Antonio de Andrade*, a Portuguese
Jesuit, determined to enter Tibet through India.   It
is claimed that he was the first Christian missionary
to cross the Himalayas, and on Easter Day, 12th
April, 1626, he laid the foundation stone of the first
Christian Church in Tibet at a little town on the
upper Sutlej River.   He died eight years later, with
symptoms of poisoning.

Stephen Cacella, another Portuguese Jesuit, reached
Shigatse in 1627, and died in that town in 1630.   In
1643 the Tibetan Jesuit Mission issued an eloquent
appeal to Europe for support to enable them to continue
their work :

" Want of men and money has compelled us to give
up the Mission, but we cannot leave the country
entirely to itself.   Great sacrifices have been made.
Brother *Bento de Goes* has died in discovering it.
After him Fathers Cacella and Diaz have passed away—
let us not be less generous ! The people are worth it ! "
But the appeal was unheeded, and in the West the
daring enterprise was soon forgotten.

Twenty years later two monks, *Johann Grueber*
and *Albert D'Orville*, made a prolonged journey through
Tibet from China to Nepal.   They visited Lhasa in
1661.   Worn out by the hardships of the way D'Orville
died at Agra in 1662 : " Midway upon his journey
between China and Europe he departed for his heavenly
home."

During the eighteenth century various Capuchin
friars travelled freely between Calcutta and Lhasa.
They founded a mission in Lhasa which was carried
on from 1715–1733.   Attempts were made to revive
it, but it finally collapsed in 1745.   It was during this
time that *Hippolyte Desideri*, another Jesuit priest,
spent several years in Lhasa (1716–1721).   In the
judgment of Sven Hedin, Desideri was " one of the
most brilliant travellers who ever visited Tibet."

---

* *Contemporaries of Marco Polo.*   Edited by M. Komroff, p. 244.

The collapse of the Capuchin Mission in 1745 marked the close of all attempts at settled missionary work in Tibet. Efforts have been made to reach the capital, but the proceeding has always been attended by much danger. For instance, in 1898 two Dutch missionaries, Mr. and Mrs. Rijnhart, set out from the Kokonor for Lhasa. Rijnhart was murdered on the Upper Mekong, and his wife only escaped with great difficulty into Szechwan.

Thus from the beginning of the nineteenth century Tibet became the Great Closed Land.

CHAPTER VI.

On the Borderland of Tibet

A GLANCE at the map will show that Tibet is surrounded by a long mountainous frontier. Starting from the north it runs southward along the borders of the three Chinese provinces of Kansu, Szechwan and Yunnan. Turning westward towards India, it skirts the northern frontiers of Burma and Assam, finally reaching Kashmir by way of Bhutan, Sikkim and Nepal. Beyond, to the north, lies Chinese Turkistan.

Thus, speaking broadly, Tibet lies midway between China and India, and from the political standpoint these are the powers with which it has to reckon. The situation is further complicated by the presence of Russia in the background.

What then is the missionary situation throughout this vast borderland ? To what extent is Tibet a " closed land " ? How far are the Tibetans being affected by the work of missions in neighbouring lands ?

From the side of India Tibet *is* a " closed land " to missions. The situation is far more promising on the Sino-Tibetan frontier. In 1928 two missionaries received official permission from Lhasa to travel through Tibet. It took them ten months to march from Sining in Kansu to Leh in Kashmir. It was a hazardous expedition, and the travellers had much to endure. On one occasion they went for twenty-seven hours without anything to drink ; when they did find water it was covered with a green scum and swarming with mosquitoes, but such things seem almost tolerable when one is consumed by raging thirst. One of the great difficulties in travelling through such desert country was the frequent loss of animals due to lack of grass and water. Everywhere the missionaries had entire freedom to preach and distribute the Scriptures, and they found the people friendly and approachable.

I.

(i.)

Kansu-Tibetan Border.

Sining, the city of " Western Peace," bears a name out of keeping with its history. Certainly the city has suffered severely in the miseries which have accompanied the Muhammadan rebellions. Its sufferings were especially severe during the Rebellion of 1895. The *China Inland Mission* early recognized the importance of Sining as a missionary centre, standing as it does where four wide valleys meet, and easily accessible to the Tibetan traders who come to it from beyond the mountains. Tibetans visit the city freely, bringing with them for sale their loads of firewood, butter, wool, and other products. Not far away, among the western mountains, there are some twenty lamaseries, and red and yellow lamas often mingle with the crowds in the streets of Sining.

Since 1885 pioneer work in Sining has been carried on by Mr. Cecil Polhill, of the China Inland Mission, and many others on whose hearts God has laid the burden of the great " closed land." Since 1923 a very definite step forward has been taken by the purchasing of premises now known as the Tibetan Gospel Inn, where there is free accommodation for a large number of guests. Plenty of stable room is provided, for nearly all Tibetans who visit the city are mounted on camels, yaks, mules, horses or donkeys. There is also a kitchen in which the guests cook their own food. The chief feature of the Inn is the Preaching Hall, a large room which will seat about fifty people in comfort. Since the opening of this building in December, 1923, the Tibetans have gradually overcome their first suspicions, and, especially from November to April, the Inn has often been overcrowded. The Tibetan evangelists, Mr. Tong and Mr. Feng, are kept busy preaching and teaching and distributing tracts.

Among the many Tibetan lamaseries near Sining, that of Kumbum, just over twenty miles distant, ranks as second or third to Lhasa in importance. It contains three thousand six hundred lamas, many of whom have visited the Gospel Inn. At the great Butter Festival, which takes place on the fifteenth day of the first Chinese month, there are always splendid opportunities for preaching the Gospel at Kumbum itself.

A number of Tibetans have already professed faith in Christ. The first to become interested in the Gospel was Chi-Fah-chia. The lamas who own the land on which he lives, have beaten him unmercifully for his refusal to continue idolatrous practices. On more than one occasion he has been imprisoned in the lamasery, chained to the ground in such a way that all night long he could neither sit down nor stand upright. Instead of the great prayer flag which has hung in the middle of his courtyard ever since he can remember, he has allowed the missionary to hang up another flag of the same length,* but instead of the Tibetan prayer " Om mani padme hum " the words of Mark i. 15 are inscribed on it : " The Kingdom of God is at hand ; repent ye and believe the Gospel."

In 1927 there were two rather remarkable conversions ; here is the story of one of them. A man who lives on the other side of Lake Kokonor had been staying at the Inn for some weeks and attending the Tibetan services, though this attendance is quite optional. At the end of one of the evening services he left his seat and came to the front. Taking his *khata* (scarf of blessing) in both hands he presented it to the God of Heaven, " for," he said, " Thou art the true God, and I will serve Thee to the end of my days." After some time this old man of seventy returned to his home in Tibet, where he will most certainly have to face the severest persecution.

In May, 1927, the foreign missionaries had to leave Sining, and the work was left in the hands of the Chinese and Tibetan evangelists. In 1928, however, the missionaries had scarcely returned to Sining

---

* Twenty feet.

before the Muhammadan Rebellion caused great tension in the neighbourhood : " Country people flocked into the walled cities, and city people sought refuge in mountain caves." The country side was swarming with armed robbers.

Up till the year 1927 the *Christian and Missionary Alliance* in this province was working amongst Chinese and Tibetans at ten stations and ten out-stations. At that time this Society had a staff of thirty-nine missionaries and fifty-four native workers. There were thirteen organized churches, with a total membership of six hundred and thirty-two. Enquirers were numerous, and, on an average, sixteen were baptized every year.

For thirty-five years this work had been going on, and it had been greatly blessed. Then came the disturbances of 1927 and the foreign missionaries had to withdraw, leaving the mission in the hands of three Chinese leaders.

During 1928 the foreign missionaries began to return to Kansu. It is the policy of this mission to press forward into unevangelized areas, and plans which had already been made for entering Tibet before 1927 were taken up again in 1928. The Chinese side of the work is being handed over to the Chinese Church, leaving the missionaries free for Tibetan work. The extension of the latter work is being planned from two new centres. The old Tibetan work at Labrang, Lupasi and Heh-tsao is being re-opened, while work among Chinese and Tibetans is being carried on at Hochow and Choni.

The Christian and Missionary Alliance has handed over the two stations of Paoan and Rungwa to the *Swedish Assemblies of God*, and some Tibetan work is being done there. The General Council of the *Assemblies of God* has work among the Tibetans at Minchow, Labrang and Tangar, with a staff of five workers.

This steady faithful work of peace is being carried on under most disturbed conditions. In Central Kansu there has been no rain for four years. The fertile region which produces wheat has become a desert. In one town the population has been reduced from sixty thousand to three thousand. Several foreign relief workers have died from typhus.* All these troubles have been accentuated by the Muhammadan Rebellion of 1928. This revolt affected Central and Western Kansu. It is believed that at least two hundred thousand people have died as a direct result of the fighting. Disease and famine have followed in the wake of the Rebellion, leaving a trail of desolation behind them. People have tried to stay their hunger with oil-cake, leaves, bark, roots and grass. Many persons have died from starvation, and in some places dogs and wolves have feasted on the children thrown outside the city walls. The rebels have sacked and burned the Tibetan monastery of Choni, destroying at the same time the only set of wooden printing blocks of the Tibetan classics in North-Eastern Tibet. The rich monastery of Labrang was seized and looted. The rising has now been subdued, and many malcontents have fled to the mountains.

At the close of the Rebellion, the Nationalist Government in Nanking decreed that the Sining district or circuit is to be carved out of Kansu Province and added to Tsinghai (Kokonor). Sining itself is to be the capital of the new province. Evidently, in future the Chinese Government hopes to exercise more than its present nominal suzerainty over Kokonor. If these hopes are realized, it is probable that this whole region will become far more open to the Gospel than it is at present.

(ii.)

Szechwan-Tibetan Border.

Tatsienlu is a centre of Tibetan work under the *China Inland Mission*. Owing to recent political changes this city is now the capital of the specially administered district of Chwanpien, which has ceased

---

* *The Times*, 30th July, 1929.

to form an integral part of the Province of Szechwan. Besides a large number of aboriginal tribes, many of whom are unknown by name to Europeans and have never yet been reached with the Gospel, Chwanpien also contains a very large, if somewhat floating, Tibetan population. Tatsienlu is the great tea centre on the Tibetan frontier, and from all parts of Tibet traders come there for this precious commodity. From 1897, when the station was first opened, attempts have constantly been made to reach these people, but difficulties, due to the uncertain political conditions, have made the work less fruitful than had been hoped.

Mr. J. Huston Edgar, an Australian member of the Mission, who is a born explorer as well as a keen evangelist, has met with most amazing adventures during his long itinerations in this territory. He sums up one year's work as follows : " Sold and distributed a hundred and two thousand tracts in Tibetan, fifty thousand books in Tibetan, and another 21,500 books in Chinese, making a total of 173,500 copies." In order to achieve these results he spent a hundred and eighty-one days away from home, travelled nearly a thousand English miles on mountainous tracts, and thirty times he reached an altitude varying from fourteen thousand five hundred to sixteen thousand feet. Dangers from wild animals, dangers from the fierce dogs which surround every nomad encampment, and dangers from robbers, were an almost daily experience. He bivouacked in the pouring rain among these precipitous hills, spent one night in drenching rain in a bog at an altitude of fourteen thousand feet, slept for six nights in soaked bedding, and for eight days wore drenched clothing. To crown all he suffered from a poisoned foot, which kept him in bed for a week and hampered him for a month, but through this delay he was able to place twenty-six thousand portions of Christian literature in the hands of lamas and other Tibetans.

In the space of twelve months this daring servant of God was able to visit the districts of no less than sixteen large lamaseries with a total of fifteen thousand priests. In spite of much opposition there are several outstanding features which enable us to glorify God on his behalf. The abbot of the lamasery at Atuntze promised that he would do all he could to circulate the Gospels which Mr. Edgar had given him. The abbot of the lamasery at K'ongyu told him that he had been spending a part of the night in prayer for him, pleading for his safety, while the high priest of the region of Tantong gave him his blessing.

One of the most important places in the district is Litang. This town lies only two hundred miles to the west of Tatsienlu, but in order to reach it ten days of arduous travel are required; thirteen passes have to be crossed at an altitude of over fifteen thousand feet. The town of Litang has about 3,300 inhabitants and the famous lamasery contains 3,700 lamas. Mr. Edgar's last visit to this place was thoroughly successful: " Scores of encampments were visited, and in spite of baying bloodhounds and grunting yaks with tails erect, eyes ablaze, and jets of steam pouring from dilated nostrils, we were able to put large quantities of literature into the hands of nomads, lamas, and brigands."

For many years Mr. and Mrs. Cunningham have been stationed at Tatsienlu, and throughout the upheaval of the last two years they remained there, caring for the small body of Chinese and Tibetan believers, and carrying on tract distribution in the surrounding neighbourhood.

An evangelistic service for Tibetans is held on Sunday afternoons. One of the great difficulties of preaching to Tibetans is that they have never been trained to sit for more than one minute in one position, or accustomed to listen for any duration beyond sixty seconds ! Mr. Edgar writes : " I have prepared a great number of addresses in the Tibetan language, which I have memorized very carefully. An address lasts for about five minutes; that is about as much as they will endure." This explains his statement that on one day he preached twenty-five times, and that within two years he delivered seventeen hundred addresses.

From the station of Batang, established in 1908, Tibetan work is carried on by the *United Christian Missionary Society (Disciples of Christ)*. That the work is hard is indicated by the fact that in 1926, even before the recent troubles, there were no baptisms. There are fourteen native workers, amongst whom there are two evangelists and ten teachers. Some medical work is being attempted with the assistance of Chinese medical workers. In a field where it is possible to reach fifty thousand people, this Mission is making a noble effort to carry on work under exceedingly difficult conditions.

(iii.)

Yunnan-Tibetan Border.

South of Szechwan the western province of Yunnan forms a kind of wedge between Burma and the rest of China. The narrow end of the wedge touches the Tibetan border. The whole of the frontier is marked by wonderful mountain scenery. Here in Yunnan there is a wealth of beauty in the flowers that bloom in its remotest regions. Indeed, this province contains some of the finest scenery in the world. French Roman Catholic missionaries live in some of these isolated valleys, shut off from all contact with the outer world during many months of the year. Their work, however, is mainly among the aboriginal tribes and does not affect Tibet.

No Protestant mission has taken up work among the Tibetans along this frontier. The country is mountainous and the villages are built at an altitude which varies from six thousand to eight thousand feet above sea level. There are many aboriginal hill tribes, and the larger cities have a small resident population of Tibetan traders, who go as far as Yunnanfu where there is a Tibetan colony.

The *Pentecostal Missionary Union (The Assemblies*

of God) has four workers at Likiang, a small town situated among the hills. The work is mostly among the hill people. Tibetans frequently visit this town on their way through to Tibet, and Gospels are given to them. The work previously carried on at Atuntze has been given up. A new station has recently been opened at Weihsi, in the country which lies between the Mekong and the Yangtse by the *Tibetan Border Mission ;* at present this work is confined to the Lisu hill people.

II.

From Yunnan we pass to BURMA, for the Northern Territories of Burma meet the frontiers of Yunnan at a point where both touch Tibet. Mission work has only recently been projected on the south of this region, which embraces the Hukawng Valley and the Triangle, where the Government of India has recently been engaged in freeing the slaves and in putting an end to head-hunting among the Nagas. The population consists of Shans in Putao, and Nagas, Kachins, and other small hill tribes, many of which have not yet been brought under Government administration.

The frontiers of Tibet north of Burma and Assam are possibly the least-known parts of Asia. One or two expeditions have entered the Abor country beyond Sadiya in Assam, but the stretch of frontier known as the Sadiya and Balipara frontier tracts and the hills beyond, lying between the bend of the Brahmaputra and the Eastern frontier of Bhutan, are still a *terra incognita.* There are no missions among these frontier peoples.

BHUTAN itself is a closed land. The people speak a form of Tibetan and their religion is lamaistic Buddhism. It has only been possible to establish indirect contact with the inhabitants. It is safe to say that economically, socially and spiritually, the quarter of a million people in Bhutan are the neediest in the whole frontier region. Work has been carried on amongst those living on the Indian frontier, but with little success. The people are very apathetic and do not desire education.

The *Church of Scotland* has a Christian congregation and a dispensary on the borders of the country, which exercise considerable influence in Western Bhutan. It is principally due to the kindly personal relations of the Rev. Dr. Graham of that Mission and the present Rajah that several village schools have been carried on in Bhutan itself, and a number of boys have also received education outside its borders. The people are not, therefore, quite without a witness, but they are for the most part hard to reach, and they remain indifferent and incurious.

THE BRITISH INDIA DISTRICTS OF DARJEELING AND KALIMPONG, with what remains of the once independent kingdom of SIKKIM, form a wedge between Bhutan on the east and Nepal on the west. Here enters the road to Lhasa, and along its difficult marches communication is kept up with India. This road passes over the Jalep La (14,390 feet) in Sikkim. At Kalimpong, a most important market town on this route, one of the Church of Scotland missionaries is specially set apart for work among the many Tibetan traders who pass through the village. In addition to services for the small congregation of Tibetan Christians, there is regular preaching in that language in the bazaar. The Nepalese have overrun Sikkim, and only eight thousand of the original inhabitants, the Lepchas, remain. The Lepchas were originally animists, but the State religion is Buddhism and Tibetan influence is strong. In the north there are a number of monasteries of the Dukpa or Red-Hat sect of Tibet.

The Church of Scotland started work in Sikkim in 1880 ; it now has twenty elementary schools and small Christian communities at about twelve places. Dispensaries or dressing stations have been established at nine of these centres, where Christian Lepchas and Nepalese seek to help the villagers to combat disease.

About thirty years ago (1898) members of the *Free Church of Finland* organized evangelistic and industrial

G

work among the people in the north of Sikkim. Twenty-eight per cent. of the Christians are literate. There are to-day eleven missionaries and forty-six indigenous workers.

West of Sikkim, stretching for nearly five hundred miles, lies the beautiful well-watered land of NEPAL, a wild mountainous country containing the highest peak in the world. As mission work is forbidden in Nepal, and no possibility of communication exists for missionaries with Tibet, the door to Central Asia is closed in this direction.*

At the east end of Nepal lies the British Indian District of KUMAON, which was captured from the Gurkhas. Here mission work is carried on by the *American Methodist Episcopal Mission*, which affects to some extent the people who use the trade routes which lead over the Milam Pass to the western extremity of Tibet and the Manasorawar Lake, a sacred place of pilgrimage in Tibet, also frequented by many Indians.

Some work in the District on this side of the Milam Pass was carried on until recently by Miss Gow, late of Rajputana, who has now retired. Another interesting work for Bhotiyas and Tibetans was that carried on for a number of years by Dr. Martha Sheldon, of the Methodist Episcopal Mission in Dharma Bhot. The sphere of her work lay in the valley of the Kali Ganga, beyond which lie the mountains of Nepal. Here at Dharchula and Tarkot in the winter, and at Sikha in the warm weather, she carried on medical work. Several attempts made by Dr. Sheldon to work in Tibet were fruitless owing to the opposition of the authorities.

Dr. Sheldon died in 1912, and for sixteen years the work has lapsed. In 1928, however, it was reopened by the Rev. and Mrs. E. B. Steiner. A small Christian community still survives as a proof of the enduring nature of the work already done.

There are other unevangelized valleys which also

---

* The position of Sikkim in relation to Nepal, Bhutan and Tibet, is unique, and by strengthening the work here much might be done to prepare and send workers into these lands.

abut on Tibet, but as they are quite cut off from the north by the barrier of mountains they belong to India's problem. The same may be said of the people of the neighbouring Tehri Garhwal State, where there is a small medical work at the capital, Tehri, under the care of Dr. Vrooman of the *Tehri-Anjuman Mission*.

As we travel westwards along the Himalayas the next approach to Tibet is by way of the SUTLEJ VALLEY, passing through Simla and thence through the Bashahr State via Poo and over the Shipki Pass. This is called the Hindustan-Tibet road, and down it came Dr. Sven Hedin from Srinagar in Kashmir, after completing his journey through Western Tibet.

For many years the *Church Missionary Society* had a missionary at Kotgarh, forty miles north of Simla. The missionaries of this Society and the Baptist missionaries from Simla often visited the upper Sutlej Valley villages of Bashahr and Kunawar. Both these Missions have now withdrawn. At one time the *Moravian Mission* had work at Chini and Poo, close to the Tibetan frontier ; the Chini work was handed over to the *Salvation Army* and finally abandoned, and recently the Poo work has also been closed. The Tibetan-speaking people of this Valley are very poor and ignorant, and, in spite of all attempts to reach them, there are no Christians there to-day.

During the season when the Shipki Pass is open, lamas and travellers pour down the Sutlej Valley, bringing ponies and wool. They can be seen in hundreds along the road, the men clad in their dirty red garments and the women with elaborately plaited hair. They listen to the preaching, but save for the occasional purchase of a Gospel they seem to be quite indifferent to all that is said. Large numbers gather at the Rampur Fair, where there is a Tibetan temple which was erected by one of the recent Rajas of Bashahr who was himself a Hindu.

There are workers associated with the *Christian Missions in Many Lands* in Dagshai, who go among the hill peoples, with whom Tibetan traders carry on business.

Dr. Watson, of the Leper Asylum at Sabathu, Simla District, superintends the work of the colporteurs of the *National Bible Society of Scotland*, who meet with the Tibetans coming to the Simla Hills during the summer. Gospels are continually being distributed and in this way the Message is conveyed in their own language.

On the west of the upper Valley of the Sutlej lies the high mountainous district of SPITI, through which the river of that name flows to join the Sutlej. The villages are mere hamlets, and shelter about three thousand people. The average height of the Valley above sea level is eleven thousand feet ; it is surrounded by mountain peaks, some of which rise to a height of twenty-three thousand feet. This is one of the most inaccessible parts of the British Empire. Government is conducted through the local chief—the Nono of Spiti. These people are strict Buddhists, and, except for occasional visits from Moravian missionaries who used to pass through Spiti on their way from Poo (which is now closed) to their station at Kyelang in Lahoul, they have never heard the story of the Gospel. They remain to-day unreached.

Still further west we cross the high passes into LAHOUL, which, with Spiti, forms the frontier part of the Kangra District of the Punjab. The land of the Chandra-Bhaga Rivers came into the possession of the British in 1846. It has been the theatre of many contending forces—Buddhism from Ladakh and Hinduism from Kulu—and to-day Buddhism is the principal religion of the people. The road to the north runs over the Lingti Pass to British Tibet (Ladakh). The Moravian Mission has worked since 1854 at Kyelang, the meeting place of the Chandra and Bhaga Rivers, and has won a few converts. The Christians in the Kyelang congregation, however, are mainly from Ladakh.

Beyond Lahoul, with its eight thousand people, lies the CHAMBA STATE, the northern district of which is inhabited by some Buddhists, who number only about five hundred, and among whom no Christian work is done. The frontier countries of Chamba, Kashmir and Jummu are mainly occupied by Hindus and Muhammadans. The Church of Scotland and the Church of England carry on work in these States.

In Northern Kashmir, however, there is a Buddhist population of about thirty-eight thousand in LADAKH, where the *Moravian Mission* has worked for over fifty years. To-day at Leh and Kalatse there is a Christian community of one hundred, half of whom are communicants. Indifference, ignorance and self-satisfaction are found everywhere, and the work calls for the highest kind of Christian courage. Organized medical work is carried on, and leprosy is being treated on modern lines. There are several schools for boys and girls, but no keenness to learn. Two women members of the *Central Asian Mission* are at present visiting the Moravians at Leh, in order to get some insight into work among Tibetan-speaking people.

BALTISTAN, which lies to the west of Ladakh, also forms part of Northern Kashmir. It is an extremely mountainous country, and one of great interest from the geographical point of view. The people are very poor and ignorant; in winter they suffer much from cold and hunger. Many of their villages are built in remote valleys, high up among the mountains, which are most difficult to reach. Skardu, the capital, is a scattered collection of houses, perched high up upon a rock above the Indus, at a height of 7,250 feet above the sea.

Two workers of the Central Asian Mission live among the Muslims in Skardu and its neighbourhood, where two schools have been established. Forty miles north-west of Skardu lies a group of villages at Rondu, which has been reported as a suitable centre for medical work. These are but small efforts in such vast territories. The interesting feature of the work of these two Missions is that it lies across the great route from India to Central Asia, from Kashmir to Kashgar and beyond. This road passes near Skardu and goes on to Gilgit, where the British Government has a military post.

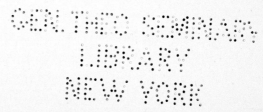

On the south side of the Karakoram Range, lie the little countries of the HUNZA and NAGAR peoples, whose true origin has long been a puzzle to ethnologists. They claim descent from Alexander the Great, and are Muslims of the Mulai sect, owing allegiance to the Aga Khan, though religion plays only a small part in their daily lives. When travellers to Kashgar pass this way visits are usually paid to the chiefs of Hunza and Nagar. The occupation of these people used to consist in raiding the caravans passing along the Leh-Turkistan road, but this has now been completely stopped, and the States, which are very poor, receive a subsidy from the Indian Government. No missionary work exists either at GILGIT or in the HUNZA-NAGAR country.

The frontier now leads into the wild valleys and passes of the Hindu Kush Mountains, a region known as KOHISTAN, which lies partly in Kashmir, partly in the Swat and Chitral areas of the North-West Province of India, and partly in Afghanistan. Little is known of these regions and neither traveller nor missionary has penetrated into their wilds.

There is a good deal of coming and going over the passes which lead from Afghanistan to Russian Central Asia, but, as Christian missions can make no approach through the closed land of Afghanistan to the lands of Central Asia, that way is closed and barred. Yet we have the story of how the Nestorian Church in the sixth century passed up through Persia and Afghanistan and penetrated to the heart of Central Asia. It may be that a day will come when this may also be possible for the Church of the twentieth century.

There is, however, one Christian messenger which is stealing into Tibet from the borderlands ; the Christian New Testament. The attractively printed Gospels—including one edition printed on native paper exactly like a Tibetan Buddhist Scripture—are continually finding their way over the border. There is a constant coming and going of Kashmiri merchants, Balti traders, Punjabi shop-keepers, religious mendicants and devotees from India as well as from Tibet,

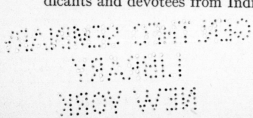

highlandmen from Ladakh and Lahoul, and even from Nepal. For all these Christian Scriptures are available. *Kashmiri, Chambiali, Kumaoni, Garhwali, Kanauri, Ladakhi*, three forms of *Lahuli, Nepali*, all have the Bible in whole or in part. We have reason to believe that books in all these tongues have actually entered Central Asia. *Arabic, Persian* and *Pashtu* are also heard over their own borders, both north and south, and in all three complete Bibles are ready for the reader. Both the *British and Foreign Bible Society* and the *National Bible Society of Scotland* are supplying the Scriptures to the missionary societies and individuals who are carrying on the work of Bible distribution along the borders of Tibet.

One of the most forceful means of spreading the knowledge of the true God to this dark corner of God's earth is, without doubt, His own Word. It is the silent missionary as well as the ubiquitous missionary and the permeating instructor. In the Bible Societies with their translations and their attractive publications, the Christian Church has at her hand what *The Times* called the gift which is in itself good, and the giving of which is perfect.

Along this extensive frontier the points of missionary contact are still few and feeble, and the strongholds of indifference and ignorance can only be broken down by faith and prayer. The call of dire need is overwhelming and constitutes a perpetual challenge to the Christian Church.

CHAPTER VII.

The Challenge

DURING the summer of 1924 the undaunted, though baffled members of the Everest Expedition returned home to tell their tale of courageous effort launched against the insuperable difficulties of the Himalayan conquest. The party was not complete, for two of its number had vanished, last seen alive silhouetted on the sky line near the summit of the impregnable mountain peak.

One who went as far as he dared in a vain attempt to track his two companions, speaks of the cold indifference with which Everest looked down on him and howled derision at his feeble attempt to wrest from it the secret of his friends' disappearance. Even as he turned back to join the camp, he realized that he had touched that line beyond which, if a man step, he must ever be led on, and regardless of all obstacles press towards that most sacred and highest peak of all.

Everest is a fitting symbol of the seemingly insuperable difficulties which confront the Central Asian missionary. The Himalayan Range is but one of the obstacles which combine to guard the land from conquest by the pioneer band. He who would enter must first sit down and count the cost, measuring his own resources of strength, endurance, time and money, and take counsel whether he be able with ten thousand to meet him that cometh against him with twenty thousand.

Nature has contributed her full quota of defence, for on the east lie deserts which are torrid or icy according to the season, whose limitless sands may only be crossed at the expense of life itself, and whose caravan routes are strewn with bleaching bones. To the south are unbroken ranges, whose few accessible passes are only grudgingly open to travellers for a few months in the year before fresh snows again block the way. On the north are the wide waterless steppes of Siberia, whose distances and dangers spell terror to the traveller.

Before the birth of Christ the Chinese historians were indicating in detail the various routes which transected the lands lying beyond their own western border. In spite of some development in railway and motor transport along the frontiers, in most of the countries described in this book the only means of transit is by cart, or camel, or on horseback. In these regions no progress in modes of travel has been made in the course of the centuries, and the stages described by Marco Polo are still followed by the weary traveller. It takes three months to traverse the trade route which connects Kucheng in Sinkiang with Peking, seventy-five days to cover the distance between Khotan and the Siberian frontier, and ninety-four days to travel from Kashgar to Suchow.

The expenditure of time and money, the demand on physical strength, the dangers from robbers, from hunger and thirst, involved in these long journeys over burning deserts, dangerous rivers or lonely waterless steppes, are some of the obstacles which must be overcome by the missionary who would seek to preach Christ in any one of the countries described in this survey.

As though in league with nature, the Governments of these lands, which are at variance on so many points, are at one in the determination to exclude the disturbing Christian missionary from a territory which all tacitly acknowledge may yet be the *Champs de Mars* of the nations.

Only those who have attempted to penetrate these fastnesses know how many obstacles block the road. Conflicting interests, international suspicion and the spirit of fear, inspire unreasoned action and astigmatic policies on the part of diplomatic Governments. How slow is man to recognize that in the coming of the Kingdom of Christ lies the peace of the world, and that apart from His dominion the air will always be alive with rumours and with the reports of those wild and foolish deeds that men perform when under the domination of fear.

Throughout the centuries statesmen and generals have coveted the control of the trade routes of Asia, knowing that great power would lie in the hands of any ruler who could dominate these strategic lines of communication. What spirit of blindness can have possessed the Christian Church for so many centuries, that she has failed even to detect that the same arteries which circulated the reports of Alexander's victories, the advance of Genghiz Khan, of Chien Lung's battles, of the progress of the great European War, and of Russia's bloody revolution, might be used to carry the knowledge of the Evangel of the Prince of Peace to places which, at this hour, are still closed to the Christian missionary.

A few Christian missionaries have overcome the initial difficulties presented by the combined forces of man and nature, and have secured entrance to the lands which lie enclosed within these formidable barriers. Then it is that the icy, sterile opposition of Islam meets their ardour and enthusiasm with cold derision and confident security : " If any man dare to oppose us he shall be swallowed up as surely as were the serpents of the magicians swallowed by the rod of Moses." Then also they encounter the paralysing atmosphere of Lamaism, well called the " Blight of Asia," which includes the teaching and practices of a debased Buddhism permeated by the obscenities of Tantric sex symbolism, and the demonism of the primitive Bon worship.

The Everest expedition did not return with the triumphant knowledge of having reached the summit. If the two brave men who so tragically vanished from sight on that May morning gained their objective, they did not return to tell the story. Yet so much was accomplished that every subsequent attempt will be on known ground until the explorers are within a few hours' climb of the summit.

The missionaries of Central Asia are still wrestling with the initial difficulties of pioneer advance in unknown lands amongst people of many a strange tongue. Their reports speak rather of a great attempt than of actual achievement, and some of these pioneers are working in such great isolation that they are lost from view by the watchers at the base.

At some future time the adventure which is costing them so much may have become an easy undertaking for their successors, but these will advance over the road traced by the vanguard, which, having opened the way, will have proved the possibility of the undertaking. Men and women, see to it that neither cowardly fear nor dastardly ease hold you back from keeping open that road which it has cost the very life of the pathfinder to make.

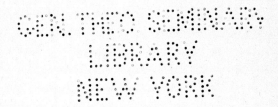

APPENDICES

INTRODUCTION : SUGGESTED POLICY OF MISSIONARY ADVANCE.

STATISTICAL SUMMARY.

STATISTICAL TABLES.

  I. RUSSIAN CENTRAL ASIA.

 II. CHINESE TURKISTAN.

III. NORTH-WEST KANSU AND KANSU-TIBETAN BORDER.

 IV. MONGOLIA.

  V. TIBET.

 VI. CHINESE AND INDIAN BORDERLANDS.

BIBLIOGRAPHY.

CHRONOLOGICAL TABLES.

INTRODUCTION

Suggested Policy of Missionary Advance

Since the last Survey was issued there has been some increase in missionary effort. This advance has been carefully reviewed in the preceding pages. The recently created Central Asia Prayer Fellowship has resulted in a more comprehensive knowledge of, and deeper interest in, these lands, and will enable the missions concerned to devise more concerted policies of advance.

The most hopeful and productive method of missionary work in the conditions which have been described is that of Bible distribution. For more than a century the Bible Society has been supplying Scriptures in the principal languages spoken within the enormous area constituting Central Asia, as well as in those tongues used on its borders. By colporteurs, missionaries, travellers, merchants, these volumes have been filtering through for many years. Its agents have regularly made long caravan tours across the Gobi, reaching not only the nomads roaming over the Desert, but leaving portions of Scriptures in monasteries and villages on and off the main trade routes. The few missionaries actually at work all agree in testifying to the value of the printed Gospels with which they are regularly supplied. They bear their testimony to the fact that this is one of the greatest contributions to the spread of the knowledge of the Gospel, even in those closed lands into which missionaries are not permitted to enter. The Word of God is not bound ; and doors closed to foreign missionaries are often open to the printed page.

It must be remembered that most of the peoples living in Central Asia speak languages like some form of Chinese, or of Turkish, or Russian, or Tibetan, or Mongolian, which are used widely outside of their own particular territory, and in all these widely-spoken languages the Scriptures, either in whole or in part, are now available. Even the more provincial tongues, such as the various dialects of Kashgar, or Kirghiz, are increasingly being enriched by books of Christian Scripture. In all the principal languages encircling Central Asia, as well as those spoken within this great tract, the Bible Society is supplying, and is always ready to supply, portions of God's Word. Travellers have told us that the number of those who are able to read is much larger than might be expected. Most monasteries and religious houses impart a certain amount of instruction, and most villages contain at least a few who are literate. To such, a new printed book in their own tongue is a wonderful experience.

The policy of extensive distribution is being steadily pursued by the British and Foreign Bible Society and by the National Bible Society of Scotland, and is profoundly influencing the whole region.

The rise of the Chinese and Indian Churches to the consciousness of their separate existence forms another great factor in the further evangelization of Central Asia. The effective co-operation of these two great Churches is essential to evangelistic advance. What is happening in the Kansu Corridor is prophetic of what may happen in Mongolia, Sinkiang and Tibet.

A third need in reviewing any policy of advance in Central Asia is that of increasing the missionary contribution of the Western Churches.

The missions now at work on the Chinese frontier need to be greatly strengthened and their work co-ordinated by mutual consultation. It is essential to carry the Chinese Church with them. The missions in Inner Mongolia, in co-operation with the Chinese Christians, can easily make a more concerted advance into the interior. The two missions at work in Northern Kashmir among the Muslim and Buddhist peoples respectively need much more help from their supporters, and a mutual plan of operations should be agreed upon, so that the very most may be made of their resources. It has been suggested that a base should be established at Srinagar, to which workers could retire for recuperation, and from which supplies could be forwarded regularly. The conditions of life are so strenuous in these regions that no great and effective work can be contemplated without such a base, which could also be a training centre. Plans of work in such regions need to be far-sighted and the workers effectively equipped if any permanent result is to be achieved.

In a peculiar way the responsibility for the evangelization of these lands must devolve on the indigenous Christians, and the contribution which missions and the Chinese and Indian Churches are especially called on to make is to equip and inspire them to undertake this arduous task.

From both the Chinese and Indian sides enterprising evangelists have sought to penetrate Tibet. Sadhu Sundar Singh has shown how difficult such approach is, but he has also proved its possibility. All these efforts are signs of promise. There is no doubt that the Church of India can do much to carry the Gospel over its frontiers. These closed lands are the natural mission field for the efforts of the Church of India and the Church of China.

In all missionary effort the controlling factor should be co-operation with these Churches, without whose aid the task cannot be completed.

Above all, the Kingdom can only truly advance through the prayers of Christian people. Closed doors will thus be opened, labourers thrust forth into this needy field, and a great harvest reaped to the glory of God and the salvation of these millions for whom Christ died.

LIST OF MISSIONARY SOCIETIES WITH THEIR ABBREVIATIONS

A.G. Foreign Missions Department, General Council of the Assemblies of God.

B.F.B.S. British and Foreign Bible Society.

C.A.M. Central Asian Mission.

C.I.M. China Inland Mission.

C.M.M.L. Christian Missions in Many Lands.

C. of S. Church of Scotland Foreign Mission Committee.

C.M.A. Christian and Missionary Alliance.

C.M.S. Church Missionary Society of Africa and the East.

F.C.F. Free Church of Finland.

H.F.M. Hephzibah Faith Mission.

K.M.B.C. Kremmer Mennonite Brethren Church (China Mennonite Mission Society).

M.E.F.B. Board of Foreign Missions of the Methodist Episcopal Church.

Mor.M. Moravian Missions.

M.P. Board of Foreign Missions of the Methodist Protestant Church.

S.A. Salvation Army.

S.A.M. Scandinavian Alliance Mission of North America.

S.M. Swedish Mongol Mission.

S.M.F. Swedish Missionary Society.

Sv.A.M. Swedish Alliance Mission. (Working in conjunction with the China Inland Mission.)

Sw.A.G. Swedish Assemblies of God.

T.B.M. Tibetan Border Mission.

T.T.M. Tibetan Tribes Mission.

U.C.M.S. United Christian Missionary Society (Disciples of Christ).

STATISTICAL SUMMARY

Countries covered in this Survey.	Area. Sq. Miles.	Population.	No. of Missions.	No. of Stations.	Mission- aries.
Russian Central Asia ..	1,612,891	14,710,378	—	—	—
Chinese Turkistan ..	550,340	2,519,579	2	5	34
Kansu*	125,450	5,927,997	6	12	22
Mongolia	1,445,000	8,098,000 (est.)	10	27	97
Tibet	470,000	2,900,000 (est.)	—	—	—
	4,203,681	34,155,954	15	44	150
Szechwan-Tibetan Border			2	2	17
Yunnan-Tibetan Border			2	2	6
Indian-Tibetan Border..			8	6	27
			23	54	200

* **Kansu :** The total area is given. There are three million Muslims in Kansu. About one-quarter of the population is in that part ascribed to Central Asia in the survey.

STATISTICAL TABLES

APPENDIX I.

RUSSIAN CENTRAL ASIA

Republics.	Area. Sq. Miles.	Population.	Chief Town.	Population.
Uzbek S.S.R.	131,410	5,270,200	Samarkand	101,400
Tadzhik Aut. S.S.R. ..	30,888	745,200	Dyushambe	
Kazak Aut. S.S.R.	1,129,347	6,530,528	Kzyl-Orda	8,466
Kara-Kalpak Aut. Area ..	43,630	303,460	Turtkul	4,252
Turcoman S.S.R.	182,630	883,549	Askhabad	47,155
Kirghiz Aut. S.S.R. ..	94,983	977,441	Kara-Kol	
	1,612,891	14,710,378		

Uzbek S.S.R. has 31 towns and 14,788 villages.
Turcoman S.S.R. has 7 towns and 2,066 villages.
The above six Republics make up the area here described as Russian Central Asia. The Uzbek and Turcoman Republics are constituent members of the Union of Soviet Socialist Republics. The Tadzhik Aut. S.S.R. is under Uzbek. The Kazak (Cossack) and Kirghiz Aut. S.S.Rs. are constituent members of the Russian Socialist Federal Soviet Republic. The Kara-Kalpak Aut. Area is under the Kazak Republic. The Oyrat Aut. Area shown on the map is in Siberia.

APPENDIX II.

CHINESE TURKISTAN (SINKIANG)

Stations.	Mission.	Missionaries.			
		Men.	Wives.	Single Women.	Total.
Urumtsi (1908)	C.I.M.	3	—	—	3
Kashgar (1894)	S.M.F.*	3	2	3	8
Hancheng (1909)	S.M.F.	1	—	1	2
Yangi-Hessar (1912)	S.M.F.	1	1	—	2
Yarkand (1897)	S.M.F.	3	1	6	10
5	2	11	4	10	25

* The Figures for this Mission are those of 1926. At present the total staff is thirty-one, of whom six are on furlough.

APPENDIX III.

NORTH-WEST KANSU AND KANSU-TIBETAN BORDER

Stations.	Mission.	Missionaries.			Total.
		Men.	Wives	Single Women.	
Sining	C.I.M. ..	2	1	—	3
Kanchow	Chinese Church	—	—	—	—
Suchow	Chinese Church	—	—	3	3
Labrang	C.M.A. ..	1	1	—	2
	A.G.	1	—	—	1
Lupasi	C.M.A. ..	—	—	—	—
Heh-tsao	C.M.A. ..	—	—	—	—
Choni	C.M.A. ..	2	1	—	3
Taochowling	C.M.A. ..	—	—	—	—
Paoan	Sw.A.G. ..	1	1	—	2
Rungwa	Sw.A.G. ..	1	1	—	2
Minchow	A.G.	1	1	—	2
	T.T.M. ..	1	1	—	2
Tangar	T.T.M. ..	1	1	—	2
12	6	11	8	3	22

APPENDIX IV.

MONGOLIA

Stations.	Mission.	Missionaries.			
		Men.	Wives.	Single Women.	Total.
Sui-Yuan District.					
Patsebolong	S.A.M. (1904)	1	1	1	3
Wangtefu, via Ningsia	,,	1	—	—	1
Kweihwating	S.A. (1918)	1	1	—	2
Pingtichuan	,,	—	—	1	1
Kweihwating	Sv.A.M. (1886)	1	1	2	4
Pao-tow-chen	,,	1	1	2	4
Saratsi	,,	3	—	4	7
Shaerhtsin	,,	—	—	—	—
Tokotoching	,,	—	—	—	—
Liang-Cheng	,,	—	—	—	—
Peh-keh-chi	,,	—	—	—	—
Chahar District.					
Fengchen	S.A.	2	1	—	3
,,	Sv.A.M.	1	1	2	4
,,	A.G. (1909)	—	—	1	1
Dolonnor	A.G.	1	1	—	2
Gashatay	,,	—	—	4	4
Chang Pei Hsien	,,	1	1	—	2
Halong-Osso	S.A.	1	1	—	2
,,	S.M.	—	—	—	—
Gulchagan	,,	2	1	1	4
Hattin-Sum	,,	1	1	1	3
Doyen	,,	—	—	2	2
Chininghsien	H.F.M. (1922)	1	1	2	4
Chotzeshan	K.M.B.C. (1923)	2	2	2	6
Jehol District.					
Jehol (1906)	C.M.M.L.	4	4	3	11
Pa Kow (1887)	,,	1	1	1	3
Ta-Tze-Kou (1885)	,,	1	1	3	5
Chao Yang	,,	2	2	2	6
Hada (1912)	,,	4	1	2	7
Sitao District.	Nil.	—	—	—	—
Mongolian Borders. (Chihli.)					
Kalgan	B.F.B.S.	1	—	—	1
,,	M.P. (1909)	2	1	1	4
,,	S.A. (1918)	1	—	—	1
27	10	36	24	37	97

APPENDIX V.

TIBET

Province.	Area. Sq. Miles.	Population.	Chief Towns.	Population.
Ü .. .. Tsang			Lhasa ⌠Shigatse ⌡Gyantse	20,000* 17,000† 5,000
To-ngari-Korsum .. .. Chang Tang .. .. Kam .. .. .. Hor .. .. .. Derge				
	470,000	2,900,000		

* Permanent Population, 12,000 ; Floating Population, 8,000.
†   ,,   ,,   12,000 ;   ,,   ,,   5,000.

APPENDIX VI.

CHINESE AND INDIAN BORDERLANDS

SZECHWAN-TIBETAN BORDER

Stations.				Missions.	Missionaries.			
					Men.	Wives.	Single Women.	Total.
Tatsienlu	..	..	..	..	C.I.M.	2	2	—	4
Batang	..	..	..	..	U.C.M.S.	6	6	1	13
2					2	8	8	1	17

YUNNAN-TIBETAN BORDER

Stations.				Missions.	Missionaries.			
					Men.	Wives.	Single Women.	Total.
Likiang	..	..	..	..	A.G.	1	1	2	4
Weihsi	..	..	..	..	T.B.M.	1	1	—	2
2					2	2	2	2	6

INDIAN-TIBETAN BORDER

District.				Mission.	Missionaries.			
					Men.	Wives.	Single Women.	Total.
Sikkim	..	..	..	..	C. of S. } F.C.F. }	4	1	6	11
Dharchula Pass (Almora)	..	..	..	M.E.F.B.	1	1	0	2
Simla Hill States	..	..	..	C.M.S. S.A. C.M.M.L.	2	1	2	5
Lahoul	..	..	..	..	Mor.M.	1	1	—	2
Ladakh	..	..	..	..	Mor.M.	2	2	1	5
Baltistan	..	..	..	..	C.A.M.	2	—	—	2
6					8	12	6	9	27

BIBLIOGRAPHY

The bibliography of Central Asia is immense, and it exists in a variety of languages. The following brief list of books in English is merely suggestive. Several of these works contain detailed lists of books. Articles in the *Encyclopaedia Britannica*, the *Journal of the Central Asian Society*, and the *Geographical Journal* are a mine of general information.*

Andrews, Roy Chapman. *Across Mongolian Plains.* 1921. (T.G.)
Andrews, Roy Chapman. *On the Trail of Ancient Man.* 1926. (T.G.)

Bartol'd, Vasily V. *Turkestan down to the Mongol Invasion.* 1928. (Second edition.) (H.)
Bell, Sir Charles Alfred. *Tibet, Past and Present.* 1924. (G.)
Bell, Sir Charles Alfred. *The People of Tibet.* 1928. (G.)
Bitton, Nelson. *Our Gilmour.* 1925. (M.)
Browne, E. G. *A Literary History of Persia.* (Volume III., Persian Literature under Tartar Dominion, 1265–1502.) 1920. (H.)
Bryson, Mary Isabella. *The Story of James Gilmour and the Mongol Mission.* 1894. [Re-issued 1928.] (M.)
Budge, Sir G. A. Wallis. *The Monks of Kublai Khan.* (M.H.)

Cable, Mildred, and French, Francesca. *Dispatches from North-West Kansu.* 1925. (M.T.)
Cable, Mildred, and French, Francesca. *The Red Lama.* 1927. (M.)
Cable, Mildred, and French, Francesca. *Through Jade Gate and Central Asia.* 1927. [An account of journeys in Kansu, Turkestan and the Gobi Desert.] (T.M.)
Candler, E. *The Unveiling of Lhasa.* 1905. (T.)
Christie, Ella R. *Through Khiva to Golden Samarkand.* 1925. (T.)
Combe, George Alexander (Editor). *A Tibetan on Tibet.* (Paul Sherap.) 1926. (G.)
Curtin, Jeremiah. *The Mongols: A History.* 1908. (H.)

Easton, John. *An Unfrequented Highway.* 1928. [Through Sikkim and Tibet to Chumolaori.] (T.)

Fox, Ralph. *People of the Steppes.* (T.G.)
Francke, A. H. *A History of Western Tibet.* 1907. (H.)

Gilmour, James. *James Gilmour of Mongolia. His diaries, letters and reports.* Edited by R. Lovett. 1892. (M.)

* G=General Information.
H=History.
M=Missions.
T=Travel.

Gilmour, James. *More about the Mongols.* 1893. [Selected by R. Lovett.] (M.)

Gregory, J. W., and C. J. *To the Alps of Chinese Tibet.* 1923. (T.)

Harrison, Marguerite E. *Asia Reborn.* 1928. (H.)
Harris, Norman Dwight. *Europe and the East.* (H.)
Haydon, H., and Cosson, C. *Sport and Travel in the Highlands of Tibet.* (T.)
Heber, A. R., and K. M. *In Himalayan Tibet.* 1926. (M.T.)
Hedin, Sven Anders. *Central Asia and Tibet.* 1903. (T.)
Hedin, Sven Anders. *Adventures in Tibet.* 1904. (T.)
Hedin, Sven Anders. *My Life as an Explorer.* 1926. (T.)
Hedley, John. *On Tramp among the Mongols.* 1906. (M.T.)
Hedley, John. *Tramps in Dark Mongolia.* 1910. (M.T.)
Howorth, Sir H. *History of the Mongols.* 1876–78. (H.)
Huc, E. R., and Gabet. (Translated by W. Hazlitt. Edited by Paul Pelliot.) *Travels in Tartary, Tibet and China.* 1844–46. 1928. (T.M.)
Hutton, J. E. *History of the Moravian Missions.* 1922. (M.H.)

Kidd, B. J. *The Churches of Eastern Christendom.* 1927. (M.H.)
Komroff, Manuel. *Contemporaries of Marco Polo.* 1928. [Travel Records of Rubruck, Carpini and Friar Odoric.] (T.M.)

Lamb, Harold. *Genghis Khan : The Emperor of all Men.* 1928. (H.)
Lamb, Harold. *Tamerlane : The Earth-Shaker.* 1928 ? (H.)
Landon, Perceval. *Lhasa.* 1906. (T.)
Lansdell, Henry. *Russian Central Asia.* 1887. (T.M.)
Lansdell, Henry. *Through Central Asia.* 1887. (T.M.)
Latourette, K. S. *A History of Christian Missions in China.* 1929. (M.)
Lattimore, Owen. *The Desert Road to Turkestan.* 1928. (T.)
Le Coq, Albert. *Buried Treasures of Chinese Turkestan.* 1928. (T.)
Le Strange, Guy. *Lands of the Eastern Caliphate.* 1896. (G.)
Le Strange, Guy (translated by). *Clavijo's Embassy to Tamerlane,* 1403–1406. 1928. (H.)

Macdonald, David. *The Land of the Lama.* 1929. (G.)
Mingana, Alphonse. *The Early Spread of Christianity in Central Asia and the Far East.* 1925. [Reprint from the Bulletin of John Rylands Library, Manchester. Volume IX., No. 2, July, 1925.] (H.M.)
Morden, W. J. *Across Asia's Snows and Deserts.* (T.)

Nairne, W. P. *Gilmour of the Mongols.* 1924. (M.)

Rickmers, W. R. *The Duab of Turkestan.* 1913. (G.T.)
Rijnhart, Susie Carson. *With the Tibetans in Tent and Temple.* 1901. (M.T.)
Rockhill, W. W. *The Land of the Lamas.* 1891. (G.)

Robson, E. I. *Alexander the Great.* 1929. (H.)

Ross, Sir E. Denison. *Aldred Lectures. Journal of the Society of Arts,* 20th and 27th September, 4th and 11th October, 1929. (H.)

Ross, Sir E. D., and Skrine, F. *The Heart of Asia.* 1899. [A History of Russian Turkestan and Central Asian Khanates.] (H.)

Shah, Sirdar Ikbal Ali. *Westward to Mecca.* 1928. (T.)

Shelton, Dr. Albert. *Pioneering in Tibet.* 1926. (M.)

Skrine, C. P. *Chinese Central Asia.* 1926. (G.)

Stein, Sir Marc Aurel. *Sand-buried Ruins of Khotan.* 1903. [Chinese Turkestan.] (T.)

Stein, Sir Marc Aurel. *The Thousand Buddhas.* 1921. [Ancient Buddhist Paintings from the Cave-Temples of Tun-huang on the Western Frontier of China.] (T.)

Stein, Sir Marc Aurel. *Ruins of Desert Cathay.* 1912. [Central Asia and West China.] (T.)

Stein, Sir Marc Aurel. *Serindia.* 1921. (T.)

Stein, Sir Marc Aurel. *Innermost Asia.* 1928. [A detailed report of explorations in Central Asia, Kansu and Eastern Iran.] 4 volumes. (T.)

Stewart, John. *Nestorian Missionary Enterprise.* 1928. (M.H.)

Sykes, Ella C., and Sir Percy M. *Through Deserts and Oases of Central Asia.* 1920. (T.G.)

Taylor, Mary Geraldine. *The Call of China's Great North-West.* 1923. [Kansu and Beyond.] (M.)

Vambéry, Arminius. *The Story of my Struggles.* 1904. (G.T.)

Waddell, L. A. *The Buddhism of Tibet or Lamaism.* 1895.

Wessels, C. *Early Jesuit Travellers in Central Asia,* 1603–1721. 1924. (T.M.)

Younghusband, Sir Francis. *Peking to Lhasa.* 1925. [A compilation.] (T.)

Younghusband, Sir Francis. *The Epic of Mount Everest.* 1926. (T.)

Yule, Sir Henry (Translator and Editor). *The Book of Ser Marco Polo.* 1903. (T.)

Zwemer, S. M. *Across the World of Islam.* 1928. (M.)

CHRONOLOGICAL TABLE

B.C. Date.	Greece.	B.C. Date.	Palestine and Syria.	B.C. Date.	Western and Central Asia.	B.C. Date.	China.
		740–701	Ministry of Isaiah.			1120–249	Chou Dynasty.
		722	Fall of Samaria and end of Israel as a Kingdom.				
621	Draco codifies laws of Athens.	626	Call of Jeremiah.			604	Birth of Lâo-Tsze.
		621	Reforms of Josiah.				
		592–570	Ezekiel.				
		586	Jews exiled to Babylon.	560 (c)	Birth of Buddha.	551	Birth of Confucius.
				539–529	Cyrus rules Persia.		
				538	Cyrus' Edict for the Return of the Jews.		
				532	Buddha renounces the world.		
				521–485	Darius I rules Persia.		
490	Battle of Marathon.	520	Haggai and Zechariah advocate re-building of Temple.				
480	Battle of Salamis.			485	Accession of Xerxes I.	479	Death of Confucius.
480–338	The " Great Age " of Greece.						
431–404	Peloponnesian War.			477 (c)	Death of Buddha.		
427	Birth of Plato.			464–424	Artaxerxes I.		
401	Xenophon leads Retreat of Ten Thousand.	458	Return of the Jews under Ezra.				
399	Death of Socrates.						
384–322	Aristotle.						
347	Death of Plato.						
359–336	Rise of Macedonia.						
356	Birth of Alexander the Great.						
343–342	Alexander taught by Aristotle.						
336	Assassination of Philip of Macedonia. Accession of Alexander III.						
334	Alexander invades Asia Minor.						
333	Alexander defeats Darius of Persia at Issus.						

CHRONOLOGICAL TABLE

B.C. Date.	Greece.	B.C. Date.	Palestine and Syria.	B.C. Date.	Western and Central Asia.	B.C. Date.	China.
332	Alexander destroys Tyre, occupies Egypt, founds Alexandria.	332	Submission of the Jews to Alexander the Great.	331–324	Alexander's Campaigns.		
331	Battle of Arbela.						
330–329	Alexander invades Persia and Bactria.						
328–327	Alexander in Bactria and Sogdhiana (Bukhara). Marries Roxana. Murder of Clytus at Samarkand. Invades India.						
324	Alexander returns to Babylon.	320	Palestine under the Ptolemies.	323	Death of Alexander at Babylon.		
323	Death of Alexander.			323–129	Struggle between the Seleucids and the Parthians.		
		198	Antiochus III of Syria conquers Palestine.	(c) 265	Asoka in India and the spread of Buddhism.	249–210	Tsin Dynasty. Che Hwang-Te, the "first universal Emperor constructs roads," canals and buildings. Great Wall erected to keep out Tatars.
		168	Antiochus IV (Epiphanes) tries to suppress Jewish religion.			246	
		167	Jews revolt, led by Maccabees.				
		165	Jerusalem re-captured and Temple worship restored.			206	Beginning of the Han Dynasty.
		160	Death of Judas Maccabaeus.				
		160–142	Jonathan.				
		142–135	Simon Maccabaeus.				
146	Decline of Greece. Destruction of Corinth. Greece conquered by Rome.	142	Jews gain independency of Syria.				
		65	Pompey captures Jerusalem. Palestine becomes a Roman Province.				
		40–37	Antigonus.				
		37–4	Herod the Great.				
		6	Birth of JESUS CHRIST.				

CHRONOLOGICAL TABLE

A.D. Date.	British Isles.	A.D. Date.	Europe (Continent).	A.D. Date.	Western and Central Asia and N. Africa.	A.D. Date.	China.
		14	Tiberius, Emperor of Rome.				I-an Dynasty (to c.200 A.D.)
				26	Pilate Procurator of Judaea.		
				27	Preaching of John the Baptist.		
				29	Baptism of JESUS CHRIST. The CRUCIFIXION OF JESUS.		
43	Claudius sends Aulus Plautius into Britain.	37	Caligula, Emperor of Rome.	30–37 (?)	Conversion of Paul.		
		41	Claudius, Emperor of Rome.				
		44	Jews expelled from Rome.				
50	Defeat of Caractacus.	54	Nero.	45–46	Paul's missionary journeys.		
				56–58	Paul's detention at Caesarea.		
				58	Festus Procurator of Judaea.		
61 or 66	Revolt of Boadicaea.	59–61	Paul's Imprisonment in Rome.	59–61	Paul's Imprisonment in Rome.		
		64	Fire at Rome and persecution of the Christians.	64	Death of Paul and of Peter.	65	Buddhism introduced from India.
		64	Martyrdom of Paul and of Peter.	66	Revolt of Jews in Palestine.		
		68	Galba, Emperor.	69	Birth of Polycarp.		
		69	Otho, Vitellius, Vespasian.	70	Fall of Jerusalem (Judaea made a separate province).		
81	Agricola in Britain.	79	Accession of Titus. Destruction of Pompeii.				
		81	Accession of Domitian.				
		96	,, Nerva.				
		98	,, Trajan.				
119	Hadrian visits Britain.	117	,, Hadrian.	115	Martyrdom of Ignatius.		

CHRONOLOGICAL TABLE

A.D. Date.	British Isles.	A.D. Date.	Europe (Continent).	A.D. Date.	Western and Central Asia and N. Africa.	A.D. Date.	China.
121	Hadrian builds Wall from Solway—Tyne.			135	Destruction of Jerusalem.		
120ff	Romans fight against Picts and Scots.			135–160	Chief period of Gnostic influence.		
		138–161	Antoninus Pius.	150	Church of the East at Edessa (Urfa).		
		147–161	Marcus Aurelius co-regent.	155	Martyrdom of Polycarp.		
		177	Persecution of Christians at Lyons and Vienne.				
		180	Commodus, Emperor.	185	Pantaenus visits India.		
		193	Septimus Severus, Emperor.	c 200	Death of Irenaeus.		
				150–216	Clement of Alexandria.		
				150–222	Tertullian.		
211	Emperor Severus dies in York after expedition against Picts and Scots.			182–251	Origen.		
				200–258	Cyprian.		
		249–251	Decius, Emperor.	238	Mani teaches in Persia. (Put to death 277.)		
		250	Outbreak of Decian Persecution.				
		250–259	Fierce but intermittent persecution of Christians.	250–259	Fierce but intermittent persecutions of Christians.		
		284	Diocletian, Emperor of Rome.				
303	Martyrdom of St. Alban.	303	Diocletian Persecution.	303	Diocletian Persecution.		
		312	Edict of Milan (Toleration of Christianity throughout Empire.)	302	Gregory, the Illuminator in Armenia.		
		323	Triumph of Constantine.				

CHRONOLOGICAL TABLE

British Isles.	A.D. Date.	Europe (Continent).	A.D. Date.	Western and Central Asia and N. Africa.	A.D. Date.	China.	A.D. Date.
		Martin of Tours evangelizes France.	316-397	First General Council at Nicaea.	325		
				Abyssinian Church founded (by missionaries from Alexandria).	330		
Rome withdraws from Britain.	401-410	Ambrose (Bishop of Milan).	340-397	Severe Persecutions of Christians in Persia.	339-448		
		Ulfilas died in Bulgaria.	381	Augustine (of Hippo).	354-430		
				Chrysostom.	345-407		
Patrick in Ireland.	432			Cyril, Patriarch of Alexandria.	412-444		
Ninian in South Scotland.	432			Council of Ephesus.	431		
		Conversion of Clovis.	496	Council of Chalcedon.	451		
				Death of Nestorius.	451 c.		
				Nestorian Patriarchate set up at Babylon.	498	Nestorian Christianity reaches China.	c. 505
				Nubian Church founded.	548		
				Nestorian monks from China brought eggs of mulberry silkworms to Constantinople. Justin II makes treaty with the Turks.	(from) 551		
Columba at Iona.	567				568-569		
				Birth of Muhammad at Mekka.	569		
Landing of Augustine in Kent.	596 (?)	Pope Gregory the Great.	590-604			T'ang Dynasty.	618-907 (c)
David in Wales.	601 (d)					Christian Influence in China.	618-845
Kentigern.	603 (d)			Muhammad's Flight from Mekka to Medina (the Hegira).	622	T'ai Tsung: "One of the greatest who ever sat on the throne of China." Ruled over China Proper, Manchuria, Mongolia, North Korea, Tibet, Sinkiang, Central Asia, North India, Tongking and Annam.	627-649
Conversion of Wessex.	634			Arabs conquer Egypt and a large part of Western Asia.	634-644		
Aidan at Lindisfarne.	635-651	Boniface in Germany.	680-755				
Synod of Whitby.	664			Eastern Turks conquer Western part of Central Asia.	711		

CHRONOLOGICAL TABLE

A.D. Date.	British Isles.	A.D. Date.	Europe (Continent).	A.D. Date.	Western and Central Asia and N. Africa.	A.D. Date.	China.
735	Death of Bede.			712	Samarkand occupied.	781	Nestorian Monument in China.
				713	Building of First Mosque in Bukhara.		
		800	Charlemagne: Beginning of the Holy Roman Empire.	753	Caliphate established at Bagdad.		
806	Iona sacked by Northmen.	826–865	Anskar in Denmark and Sweden.	786–809	Haroun-al-Raschid, Caliph.	845	Edict to suppress Christianity in China.
871–901	Alfred the Great.	863 (from)	Cyril and Methodius evangelize Slavs.	904	Turks invade Transoxania.	907–960	Five ephemeral dynasties and civil wars.
						960–1275	Sung Dynasty.
1066	Norman Conquest.			1007	Keraits become Christian.		
1086	Domesday Book compiled.	1095–99	First Crusade.	1076	Seljuk Turks capture Jerusalem.		
1093	Anselm at Canterbury.	1147–49	Second Crusade.	1157	End of the Empire of the Seljuk Turks.		
		1189–92	Third Crusade.	1162–1227	Genghiz Khan. (On his death the Mongol Empire divided among his four sons.)	1216–94	Kublai Khan (Grandson of Genghiz Khan). Founded Mongol dynasty in 1275.
		1211	St. Francis of Assisi founds Franciscan Order.				
1215	Magna Carta.	1228	Emperor Frederick II captures Jerusalem.	1218–20	Conquest of Eastern Turkestan and Transoxania by the Mongols.		
		1241	Mongols conquer Poles, Silesians and Hungarians.	1244	Turks regain Jerusalem (which they held till 1917).	1245–55	Carpini and Rubruck among Mongols.
				1258	Hulagu Khan destroys Caliphate of Bagdad.		
		1265–1321	Dante at Florence.	1260–95	Travels of the Polos.	1279	Peking made Capital of China.
						1280	Kublai Khan makes Mongol power supreme in China.
1324	Birth of John Wiclif.						

CHRONOLOGICAL TABLE

A.D. Date.	British Isles.	A.D. Date.	Europe (Continent).	A.D. Date.	Western and Central Asia and N. Africa.	A.D. Date.	China.
1348-9	The Black Death.	1348-9	The Black Death.	1300	Beginning of Empire of Ottoman Turks.	1292	Beginning of Corvino's Mission.
		1358	Turks capture Gallipoli Peninsular; under Sultans Muradi (1359–89) and Bajazet (1389–1402), they overran South-Eastern Europe.	1318-30	Friar Odoric in Central Asia.	1328	Close of Corvino's Mission.
1384	Death of John Wiclif.	1369	Birth of John Huss.	1369-1405	Conquests of Tamerlane.	1368	Ming Dynasty founded.
		1414	Council of Constance.			1369	Christianity crushed in China.
		1414	Martyrdom of Huss.				
1455-85	Wars of the Roses.	1452	Birth of Savonarola.				
		1453	Turks capture Constantinople; end of Eastern Empire.				
		1483	Birth of Martin Luther.				
		1491	Birth of Ignatius Loyola.				
		1492	Moors expelled from Granada.				
		1492	Columbus discovers New World	1498	Vasco da Gama sails to India.		
		1498	Death of Savonarola.				
1505	Birth of John Knox.	1506	Birth of Francis Xavier.				
1509	Henry VIII.	1509	Birth of John Calvin.				
		1529	Turks besiege Vienna.				
		1545-63	Council of Trent.	1542	Arrival of Xavier in India.		
		1546	Death of Luther.				
		1552	Death of Xavier.				
1555-56	Latimer, Ridley and Cranmer martyred.	1556	Death of Loyola.				
		1564	Death of Calvin.				
1572	Death of John Knox.	1572	Massacre of St. Bartholomew.				
		1598	Edict of Nantes.	1602-07	Bento de Goës in Central Asia.		
				1624	Antonio de Andrada in Tibet.	1625	Nestorian monument discovered.
1611	Authorized Version of the Bible issued.			1625-40	First Jesuit Missions in Tibet.	1650	Manchu Dynasty founded.
		1685	Revocation of the Edict of Nantes.	1661-64	Second Jesuit Mission in Tibet.		

INDEX

A.

Afghanistan, 9, 27, 34, 35, 36, 77, 102.
Aga Khan, 102.
Akhal Tekke, 35.
Aksu, 11, 27, 47.
Aksu Circuit, 52.
Alai Mountains, 32.
Alashan Mountains, 60.
Alexander the Great, 9, 13, 15, 32, 102, 106.
Alexandria Eschatê, v. Farthest Alexandria.
Almalig, v. Kulja.
Altai Kirghiz, v. Kazak Kirghiz.
Altai Mountains, 11, 41, 47, 60, 72.
American Methodist Episcopal Mission, 98.
American Museum of Natural History, 59.
Amur River, 72.
Anderson, Dr., 10.
Andrade, Antonio de, 86.
Anhsi, 55.
  Protectorate of, 11.
Anglo-Russian Convention, 35.
Aral, Sea of, 34.
Armenia, 14.
Aryans, 38, 46.
Assam, 88, 96.
Assassins, The sect of, 24.
Assemblies of God Mission, 71, 91, 95, 96.
Atuntze, 94, 96.
Avetaranian, Johannes, 52.

B.

Babylon, Death of Alexander the Great at, 9.
Babylonia, Source of Manichean religion, 11.
Babylonian Influence, Traces of, 10.
Badakshan, Border-tribes of Sinkiang, 47.
Baikal, Lake, 12, 20, 72.
Balkhash, Lake, 34.
Baltistan, 101.

Baluchistan, 9.
Barkul, 44.
Barkul, Lake, 10, 44.
  „   Mountains, 43.
Bashahr, 99.
" Basmaji " Revolt, 35.
Batang, 95.
Bhotiyas, 98.
Bhutan, 88, 96, 97.
Bible Circulation :
  In North-West Kansu, 57.
  In Mongolia, 72.
  In Russian Central Asia, 40.
  In Sinkiang, 51, 72.
  In Tibet, 88, 93, 94, 102.
  Increase in Central Asia of, 73.
  Importance in Central Asia of, 111.
Bible Society,
  British and Foreign, 39, 40, 51, 72, 73, 103, 111.
  National, of Scotland, 52, 100, 103, 111.
Bogdo Khan, v. Bogdo Lama.
Bogdo Lama, 63, 64.
Bon Religion, 83, 106.
Brethren Mission :
  In Mongolia, 70, 71, 99.
  On the Borderlands of Tibet, 99.
British and Foreign Bible Society, v. Bible Society.
Buddhism, 15, 22, 23, 47, 64, 68, 96, 97, 100, 102, 112.
  v also Lamaism.
Bukhara, 9, 17, 32, 35, 36, 38, 39, 40, 77.
Burma, 88, 95, 96.
Buryat Mongols, 69, 72.

C.

Cacella, Stephen, 86.
Calcutta, 86.
Cambaluc, 15, 25, 27.
  v. also Peking.
Capuchin Mission in Tibet, Collapse of, 86, 87.
Carpini, Friar John de Plano, 24.

I

Case, Dr., 70.
Caspian Sea, 34.
Cathay (China), 25, 27, 28, 59.
Central Asian Mission, 101.
Central Asian Turkish, v. Uzbek.
Chahar, 62, 71.
Chamba State, 100.
Chambiali, 103.
Chamdo, 83.
Chan-tou, v. Turkis.
Chao Yang, 69, 70.
Chien Lung, 47, 106.
Chi-Fah-Chia, 90.
Chihli Province, 54, 72.
China, Great Wall of, 10, 27, 54, 55, 57, 59, 72, 74.
China Inland Mission, 48, 51, 52, 57, 71, 89, 92.
Chinese :
    In Sinkiang, 43, 47, 49.
    In Mongolia, 62, 64, 66, 69–73, 74·
Chinese Church, 52, 57, 74, 91, 112.
Chinese Turkistan, v. Sinkiang.
Ching Shu-jen, 45.
Chini, 99.
Chininghsien, 71.
Chita, 65.
Chitral Area, 102.
Chomolhari, 78.
Choni, 91.
    Tibetan monastery burned by rebels at, 92.
Chotzeshan, 71.
Christian and Missionary Alliance, 91.
Christian Missions in Many Lands, v. Brethren Mission.
Chuguchak 47.
" Church of the East," 18, 21.
Church Missionary Society, 99, 101.
Church of Scotland Mission, 97, 101.
Chwanpien :
    District of, 92.
    Tibetans in, 93.
Clytus, 32.
Cochrane, Dr. Thomas, 70.
Columbus, 15, 16.
Constantinople, 14.
Corvino, John de Monte, 25.
Cossack Autonomous Socialist Soviet Republic, v. Kazakstan.
Cunningham, Mr. and Mrs., 94.

D.

Dagshai, 99.
Dalai Lama, 81, 84, 85.
Damani Koh, 40.
Danish Mission, 71.
Darjeeling, 85, 97.
Decian Persecution, 18.
Desideri, Hippolyte, 86.
Dharchula, 98.
Dharma Bhot, Dr. Sheldon's work at, 98.
Diaz, Father, 86.
Diocletian Persecution, 18.
Disciples of Christ Mission, v. United Christian Missionary Society.
Djerim League, 67.
    Chinese Settlements in, 74.
Djosotu League, 67.
    Brethren Mission in, 71.
Djouda League, 67.
    Brethren Mission Work in, 71.
    Chinese Settlements in, 74.
Dnieper, 13, 61.
D'Orville, Albert, 86.
Doyen, 70.
Drepung, 81.
Dukpa, Buddhist sect of, 97.
Dyushambe, 37.
Dzungaria, 46, 61.
Dzungaris, 38.

E.

Eastern Turki, 50.
    v. also Jagatai.
Edessa, 18.
Edgar, Mr. J. Huston, 93, 94.
Enver Pasha, 35, 36.
Esztergom, 14.
Eurasian Theory in Central Asia, 16.
Evangelical Movement in Russian Central Asia, 41.

F.

Farthest Alexandria, 10.
Feng, Marshal, 74.
Feng, Mr., 89.
Fengchen, 71.
Finland, Free Church of, 97.
Franciscan Missionaries, 23, 24, 27.

G.

Garhwali, 103.
Genghiz Khan, 9, 12, 13, 14, 15–17, 24, 32, 34, 61, 65, 66, 77, 106.
Georgia, 14.
German Mennonites, 39.
Gilgit, 101, 102.
Gilmour, James, 69, 70, 74, 75.
Gobi Desert, 11, 54, 55, 59, 60, 62, 72, 111.
Goës, Bento de, 27, 86.
Gok-kand, v. Samarkand.
Golden Horde, Defeat of, 16.
Gow, Miss, 98.
Graham, Dr., 97.
Great Wall of China, 10, 27, 54, 55, 57, 59, 72, 74.
Greek Influence in Sinkiang, 10.
Grueber, Johann, 86.
Gulchagan, 70.
Gulistan Mountains, 40.
Gushi Khan, 83, 84.
Gyantse, 82.

H.

Halong-Osso, 70.
Hami, 12, 43.
Hancheng, 49, 50.
Hattin-Sum, 70.
Hedin, Sven, 86, 99.
Heh-tsao, 91.
Hephzibah Faith Mission, 71.
Himalayas, 77, 79, 86, 99, 104.
Hindu Kush Mountains, 9, 35, 102.
Hindustan-Tibet Road, 99.
Hochow, 91.
Honan, 11, 55.
Hoshut Branch, v. Mongols.
Hsiung Nu, 10, 11.
Huktuktu, v. Bogdo Lama.
Hulagu Khan, 22.
Hungary, Mongols in, 14.
Hunter, Mr. George, 48, 51.
Hunza, 102.
Hunza-Nagar, 102.

I.

Iehedzu League, 67.
Ili, 46, 47.
Ili Tartars, v. Taranchis.

India, 9, 25, 67, 84, 88.
    Trade Route to Central Asia from, 44, 48, 78.
Indian Church, Responsibility of, 112.
Iran, v. Persia.
Irish Presbyterian Mission, 70, 71.
Islam, 14, 23, 26, 39, 91, 92, 106.

J.

Jagatai, 40.
Jalep La Pass, 97.
Jehol, 62, 71.
Jerome, St., 19.
Jesuit Missionaries, 21, 86.
Jokang, Temple of, 80.
Jummu, 101.

K.

Kalatse, 101.
Kalgan, 51, 65, 70, 72.
Kali Ganga Valley, 98.
Kalimpong, 97.
Kalmuk, 51.
Kalmuk Steppes, 72.
Kalmuk Tartars, 16.
Kalmuks, 38, 47.
Kanauri, 103.
Kanchow, 12, 55–58.
Kansu, 10, 12, 27, 44, 48, 52, 53, 55, 56–58, 77, 88, 91, 92, 112.
Kansu-Tibetan Border, 89–92.
Kao, Dr., 52, 56.
Kara Kirghiz, v. Kirghiz.
Karakoram Mountains, 77, 102.
Karakorum, 12.
Karashar, 11, 47.
Kashgar, 10, 11, 33, 43–45, 48–52, 102, 105, 111.
Kashgar Circuit, 52.
Kashgar Oasis, 43, 49.
Kashgar Turkish, 51.
Kashgaria, 11, 43.
Kashgaris, 43, 49.
Kashmir, 88, 99, 101, 102.
Kashmiri, 103.
Kazak Kirghiz, v. Kirghiz.
Kazak Kirghiz, 51 (Language).
Kazaks, 46.
Kazakstan, 36.
Keraits, Conversion of King of, 20.

Kesh, 15.
Khanbalag, v. Cambaluc.
Khingan Mountains, 60, 73, 74.
Khiva, 17, 35, 37, 38, 40.
Khojend, 10.
Khotan, 10, 11, 27, 44, 105.
Khotan Circuit, 52.
Kia-Yu-Kwan, 54.
Kiev, destroyed by Mongols, 14.
Kirghiz, 12, 34, 38, 39, 47, 111.
Kirghiz Steppe, 33, 35, 36.
Kirghiz Tartars, 16.
Kohistan, 102.
Kokand, 39, 40.
Kokonor, 87, 92.
Kokonor, Lake, 90.
Kossogol, Lake, 60.
Kotgarh, 99.
Kou Wai, 54, 55.
Kremmer Mennonite Brethren Church, 71.
Kublai Khan, 15, 33, 61, 67, 83, 84.
Kuche, 11.
Kucheng, 43, 105.
Kuen Lun Range, 77.
Kulja, 25, 46, 47.
Kulu, 100.
Kumaon, 98.
Kumaoni, 103.
Kumbum, 89, 90.
Kumul, v. Hami.
Kunawar, 99.
Kushans, v. Yueh Chi.
Kuyuk Khan, 24.
Kyelang, 100.

L.

Labrang, 91.
   Tibetan Monastery looted by rebels at, 92.
Ladakh, 100, 101, 103.
Ladakhi, 103.
Lahoul, 100, 103.
Lahuli, 103.
Lamaism, v. also Buddhism, 63, 67–69, 80, 106.
Lanchow, 53, 56.
Languages of Central Asia v. also separate entries.
   Altai Kirghiz.
   Central Asian Turkish.
   Chambiali.
   Eastern Turki.
   Garhwali.
   Jagatai.
   Kalmuk.
   Kanauri.
   Kashgar Turkish.
   Kashmiri.
   Kazak Kirghiz.
   Kumaoni.
   Ladakhi.
   Lahuli.
   Manchu.
   Mongolian.
   Nepali.
   Nogai Turkish.
   Pashtu.
   Persian.
   Russian.
   Sart.
   Tartar Turkish.
   Tekke Turkoman.
   Tibetan.
   Trans-Caspian Turkish.
   Turkestani.
   Turki.
   Turkish.
   Uzbek.
Latourette, Dr., 20.
Le Coq, Dr. Albert von, 10.
Leh, 88, 101.
Lenin, 16, 17.
Lepchas, 97.
Lhasa, 77, 79–81, 84–88, 90, 97.
Liangchow, 53.
Likiang, 96.
Lingti Pass, 100.
Litang, 94.
Little Peking, v. Tunghwang.
Liu Yi, 75.
London Missionary Society, 69, 70, 72.
Lupasi, 91.

M.

Ma, General, 44.
MacDonald, David, 82.
Manas, 43.
Manas, River, 43.
Manasorawar Lake, 98.
Manchu, 51, 73.
Manchu Dynasty, 44.
Manchuria, 45, 62, 72–74.

Manchus, 44, 47, 62, 63, 67.
Mani, 11.
Manichean Religion, 11.
Manichean Influence in Central Asia, 22.
Mather, Mr. Percy, 48.
Mekong, River, 87, 96.
Merv, 20, 35, 37.
Methodist Episcopal Mission (American), 98.
Milam Pass, 98.
Minchow, 91.
Ming Dynasty, 61, 62.
Mongolia, 13, 14, 20, 22, 45, 53, 61, 62, 63, 65, 67, 69, 72, 74, 75, 112.
Mongolian, 47, 51, 69, 72, 111.
Mongolian Missions, 70, 75.
Mongol Invasions, 12, 14, 22, 23.
Mongol Parliament, 64.
Mongols, 12, 14, 16, 20, 26, 33, 38, 46, 47, 60–63, 65–69, 71, 73–75.
Moravian Mission, 99–101.
Moscow, 36, 37, 64.
    Mongolia represented at Conference of Toilers of the Far East at, 63.
    Taken by Mongols, 14.
Muhammadan Rebellion, v. Islam.
Muhammadans v. Muslims.
Muslims, 27, 35, 39, 46, 47, 51, 57, 89, 91, 92, 101, 112.
    Sufis, 38.
    Sunnites, 38, v. also Islam.
Muztagh Ata, 49.

N.

Nagars, 102.
National Bible Society of Scotland, v. Bible Society.
Nepal, 86, 88, 97, 98, 103.
Nepalese, 97.
Nepali, 103.
Nestorian Church in Central Asia, 20, 102.
Nestorian Missionaries and the Bible, 19.
Nestorian Missionaries, 18, 19, 21, 22.
Nicholas, Brother, 25.
Nogai Turkish, 51.
Nogais, 47.
North-West Province of India, 102.

O.

Odoric, Friar, 24, 85.
Ogdai, 14.
Omsk, 45.
Ordos Desert, 70.
Orkhon River, 65.
Osh, 33, 45.
Ottoman Turks, 14.
Oxus, 32, 35, 40.

P.

Pa Kow, 70.
Pamirs, The, 10, 27, 35.
Pan-Turanian Movement, 36.
Paoan, 91.
Parker, John, 70.
Pashtu, 103.
Patsebolong, 70.
Peking, 15, 25, 27, 28, 63, 105.
Pentecostal Missionary Union, v. Assemblies of God Mission.
Peoples : v. also separate entries.
    Aryans.
    Badakshan border-tribes.
    Bhotiyas.
    Buryat Mongols.
    Chan-tou.
    Chinese.
    Dzungaris.
    Hoshut Branch of Mongols.
    Hunza.
    Ili Tartars.
    Kalmuks.
    Kalmuk Tartars.
    Kara Kirghiz.
    Kashgaris.
    Kazak Kirghiz.
    Kazaks.
    Kirghiz.
    Kirghiz Tartars.
    Kushans.
    Lepchas.
    Manchus.
    Mongols.
    Nagars.
    Nepalese.
    Nogais.
    Ottoman Turks.
    Persians.
    Russians.
    Sarts.
    Szechuanese.

Tadzhiks.
Taranchis.
Tartars.
Tibetans.
Torgut Branch of Mongols.
Torgutes.
Tungans.
Turanian Turks.
Turkis.
Turkomans.
Turks.
Uigurs.
Uzbeks.
Yarkandis.
Yueh Chi.
Persia, 9, 11, 17, 18, 24, 25, 35, 39, 102.
Persian, 103.
Persians, 38.
Peshitto Version of Scriptures, 19.
Pharijong, 78, 80, 83.
Polhill, Mr. Cecil, 89.
Polo, Marco, 59, 61, 105.
Polo, Maffeo, 15.
Polo, Nicolo, 15.
Poo, 99.
Pordenone, Friar Odoric of, 24, 85.
Potala, The, 79.
Prester John, Legend of, 20.

R.

Raquette, Rev. G., 52.
Red-hat Sect of Buddhism, v. Dukpa.
Ricci, Matthew, 27, 28.
Richthofen Range, 53.
Ridley, Mr. H. F., 48.
Rijnhart, Mr. and Mrs., 87.
Roman Missions, 25, 95.
Rondu, 101.
Ross, Sir Denison, 13, 36.
Rubruck, Friar William of, 24.
Rumi, Jalal al-Din, 38.
Rungwa, 91.
Russia, 16, 17, 34, 35, 45, 48, 59, 62, 63, 65, 72, 88.
Russia, Soviet, 16, 35–37, 39, 40, 45, 63–65.
Russian, 40, 51, 111.
Russian Altai Region, 41.
Russian Central Asia, 36, 37, 46.

Russian Evangelical Movement, 40, 41.
Russian Revolution, 17, 35, 36, 106.
Russian Turkistan, v. Russian Central Asia.
Russians, 37.

S.

Sabathu, 100.
Salvation Army, 71, 99.
Samarkand, 9, 15, 17, 31, 32, 35, 37, 39
Sart, v. Uzbek.
Sarts, 38, 46. v. also Uzbeks.
Scandinavian Alliance Mission, 70.
Scotland, Church of, 97, 101.
Scotland, National Bible Society of, v. Bible Societies.
Selenga River, 65, 69.
Semipalatinsk, 45.
Serim Pon Sok, 72.
Shanghai, Bible Society Depôt at, 51, 73.
Shansi Province, 10, 55, 72, 74.
Shantung, 74.
Sheldon, Dr. Martha, 98.
Shensi Province, 74.
Shigatse, 81, 86.
Shipki Pass, 99.
Siberia, 20, 34, 43, 47, 51, 74, 105.
Sikha, 98.
Sikkim, 77, 88, 97, 98.
Silingol League, 67.
Simla, 99.
Simla District :
    Colportage work among Tibetan travellers in, 100.
Sining, 88–90, 92.
Sinkiang, 34, 42, 47, 48, 51, 52, 55, 59, 72, 105, 112.
Sino-Tibetan Frontier, Missionary Situation on, 88.
Sitao, 62.
Skardu, Work of Central Asia Mission at, 101.
Soutter, Dr., 70.
Spiti, 100.
Srinagar, 99.
Stallybrass, Edward, 69, 72.
Stein, Sir Aurel, 10.
Steiner, Rev. and Mrs. E. B., 98.
Stewart, Dr. John, 21, 22.

Suchow (Kansu), 12, 27, 54, 55, 57, 58, 105.
Sui Yuan, 62, 71.
Sutlej River, 86, 100.
Sutlej Valley, 99, 100.
Swan, William, 69, 72.
Swat Area, 102.
Swedish Alliance Mission, 71.
Swedish Assemblies of God, 91.
Swedish Missionary Society, 39, 48–52.
Swedish Mongol Mission, 70, 73.
Sykes, Sir Percy, 33.
Szechuan, 77, 87, 88, 93, 95.
Szechuanese in Kansu, 55.
Szechuan-Tibetan Border, 92, 95.

T.

Tadzhiks, 38.
Tadzhikstan, 37, 38.
Tamerlane, 9, 15, 16, 22, 23, 25, 32.
Tangar, 91.
Taranchis, 46.
Tarim River, v. Yarkand River.
Tarkot, 98.
Tartars, 16, 25, 32, 47, 59, 83.
Tartar Turkish, v. Nogai Turkish.
Tashi Lama, 81, 84.
Tashkent, 17, 35, 37, 39, 40.
Tatsienlu, 92–94.
Tehri, Medical Mission at, 99.
Tehri-Anjuman Mission, 99.
Tehri Garhwal State, 99.
Tekke Turkoman, v. Jagatai.
Tibet, 11, 24, 35, 48, 53, 62, 67, 77, 81, 84, 86, 87, 90–92, 95–99, 102, 112.
Tibetan, 51, 92, 93, 111.
Tibetan Alps, 53, 54, 58.
Tibetan Border Mission, 96.
Tibetan Converts, 90.
Tibetan Gospel Inn at Sining, 89.
Tibetan Hermits, 82.
Tibetan Jesuit Mission, Appeal to Europe of, 86.
Tibetan Laity, 82, 83, 85.
Tibetan Lamas, Conservatism of, 85.
Tibetan Tribes Mission, v. Assemblies of God Mission.
Tibetans, 10, 11, 20, 55, 56, 58, 80, 81, 88–91, 93–99.
Tien Shan Mountains, 33, 43, 72.

Tihwafu, v. Urumtsi.
Timothy, Nestorian Patriarch, 19.
Timur, v. Tamerlane.
Timur-i-Leng, v. Tamerlane.
Toghon Timur, 61.
Tong, Mr., 89.
Torgut Branch, v. Mongols.
Torgutes, 38.
Trade Routes, Strategic Importance in Central Asia of, 106.
Trans-Caspian Railway, 45.
Trans-Caspian Turkish, v. Jagatai.
Trans-Caspian Province, 35.
Trans-Caucasia, Republic of, 17.
Trans-Himalayan Caravan Routes, 44.
Transoxania, 18, 20.
Trans-Siberian Railway, 45, 65.
Tsinghai, v. Kokonor.
Tungans, 46.
Tunghwang, 10, 55, 56.
Turan, 16.
Turanian Turks, v. Turkis.
Turcoman Socialist Soviet Republic, 17, 36.
Turfan, 10, 12, 44.
Turkestani, v. Uzbek.
Turki, 46.
Turkis, 46, 47.
Turkish, 37, 38, 111.
Turkistan, 9, 18, 20, 32, 35, 36, 39, 59.
Turkistan-Siberian Railway, 36.
Turkomans, 37.
Turks, 14, 20, 33, 36, 43.

U.

Uch-Turfan, 47.
Uigurs, 11, 12, 55, 56.
Union of Socialist Soviet Republics, 17, 36, 65.
  See also Russia, Soviet.
United Christian Missionary Society, 95.
Ural-Altaic Races, 19, 37, 46.
Urga, 48, 63, 65, 72, 73.
Urumtsi, 43, 45, 47, 48, 51.
Urumtsi Circuit, 52.
Uzbek, 40.
  Gospel in, 40.
Uzbek Republic, 17, 36, 38.
Uzbek U.S.S.R, v. Uzbek Republic.

Uzbekistan, *v.* Uzbek Republic.
Uzbeks, 37, 38.

V.

Vambery, Arminius, 39.
Vasco da Gama, 15, 16.
Vrooman, Dr., 99.

W.

Wangtefu, 70.
Watson, Dr. 100.
Weihsi, 96.
Werkne-Udinsk, 65.
William of Rubruck, Friar, 24.

X.

Xavier, Jerome, Missionary at Lahore, 27.

Y.

Yam-Dok-Tso, 79.
Yang, Governor of Sinkiang, 44, 45.
Yangi-Hessar, 49, 50.
Yarkand, 10, 27, 44, 49, 50.
Yarkand River, 43.
Yarkandis, 49.
Yellow River, 15, 62, 70.
Younghusband Mission to Tibet, 84.
Yueh Chi, 10, 56.
Yuille, Robert, 69, 72.
Yule, Sir Henry, 22, 27.
Yumen, 55.
Yunnan, 77, 88, 95, 96.
Yunnanfu, Tibetan Colony in, 95.
Yunnan-Tibetan Border, 95, 96.

Z.

Zarafshan River, 17, 32.

The Survey Series

The WORLD DOMINION SURVEY SERIES attempts to describe briefly and clearly the situation in various countries as viewed from the standpoint of the Kingdom of God.

INSULINDE: A brief Survey of the Dutch East Indies. With Map.
Price 6d. (post paid, 7d.)

A BIRD'S-EYE VIEW OF LATIN AMERICA. With Map.
Price 6d. (post paid, 7d.)

THE TASK OF THE CHRISTIAN CHURCH: A World Survey. Edited by Thomas Cochrane. Price 7/6 (post paid, 8/-)
"A book which should be in the hands of missionaries, ministers, Church secretaries, Sunday School superintendents—in fact, anyone who holds any position of leadership in Christian work, whether at home or abroad."—*British Weekly.*

THE LAND OF THE VANISHED CHURCH: A Survey of North Africa. By J. J. Cooksey. With Map. Price 2/- (post paid, 2/3)
"The book is one of great, almost fascinating interest; it is wonderful how much information is crowded into its 100 odd pages."—*Missionary Review of All Nations.*

A GREAT EMANCIPATION: A Survey of Nyasaland. By W. J. W. Roome. Price 1/- (post paid, 1/2). With Map, 4/- (post paid, 4/3)
"The facts . . . brought together in this masterly statement deal with the land and its history, the people, the growth of the African Church, the missions in Nyasaland, the progress of Islam, education and the place of the Bible."—*Life of Faith.*

NIGERIA: The Land, the people, and Christian Progress. By J. Lowry Maxwell. With Maps. Stiff paper cover, 3/6 (post paid, 3/9)
Cloth boards, gilt lettered, 5/- (post paid, 5/6)
"Gives a bird's-eye view of the conditions in Nigeria from the Christian standpoint. . . . A picturesquely told story, giving a more vivid view of these things than a more elaborate and detailed description."—*U. F. S. Record.*

AN EASTERN PALIMPSEST: A brief Survey of Turkey, Syria, Palestine and Egypt. By O. Wyon. With Maps. Stiff paper cover, 2/6 (post paid, 2/9)
"Attractively written . . . full of useful information."—*Bible in the World.*

LIGHT AND DARKNESS IN EAST AFRICA: A Survey of A. E. Sudan, Uganda, Abyssinia, Eritrea, and the Somalilands. With Maps. Cloth boards, gilt lettered, 5/- (post paid, 5/6). Stiff paper over, 3/6 (post paid 3/10)
"The World Dominion Survey Series, to which this book belongs, gains immensely in its impressiveness and usefulness as it proceeds with its accounts of the influence of Christianity throughout the world."—*Times Literary Supplement.*

THE LOWLAND INDIANS OF AMAZONIA. By K. G. Grubb. With 14 Maps. Cloth boards, gilt lettered, 5/- (post paid, 5/6)
"The writer has travelled extensively in the Amazon Valley, and has acquired a very intimate knowledge of the habits and temperament of the Lowland Indians, which makes his book very interesting to all those concerned in the problems presented by those very difficult races."—*South American Journal.*

CHURCH AND MISSIONS IN MANCHURIA: A Survey of a Strategic Field. By Alexander R. Mackenzie. With Maps. Stiff paper cover, 2/6 (post paid, 2/9)
"Mr. Mackenzie knows his subject well, and gives us a clear, unbiassed statement of the work accomplished, the difficulties in the way, and the future prospects."
Belfast Witness.

THE WAY OF THE WHITE FIELDS IN RHODESIA: A Survey of Christian Enterprise in Northern and Southern Rhodesia. By Edwin W. Smith. With Maps. Cloth boards, gilt lettered, 5/- (post paid, 5/6)
"An admirable production, packed with the latest and most accurate information as to the present position and future prospects of the missionary societies labouring in North and South Rhodesia, all presented in the most statesmanlike fashion."—
Methodist Recorder.

WORLD DOMINION PRESS, 1, Tudor Street, London, E.C. 4

Recent additions to the Survey Series

THE RIVER PLATE REPUBLICS: A Survey of the Religious, Economic and Social Conditions in Argentina, Paraguay and Uruguay. By Webster E. Browning. With 3 Maps. Cloth boards, gilt lettered, 5/- (post paid, 5/6)

"A brief but very able volume. . . . It enables us to grasp the vast extent of these River Plate lands, their great economic value and the present social condition."
The Church Overseas.

CHRISTIAN PROGRESS IN BURMA. By Alexander McLeish. With Maps and Diagrams. Cloth boards, gilt lettered, 3/6 (post paid, 3/10). Stiff paper cover, 2/6 (post paid, 2/9)

"It is most interestingly written, is full of up-to-date information, and presents a stirring appeal to the Church."—*Methodist Leader.*

OTHERS WILL FOLLOW

Reprints from World Dominion,

also

Special Articles, and Short Surveys

HOW TO RID A COUNTRY OF LEPROSY. By R. G. Cochrane.

AMAZONIA AND ITS INDIAN TRIBES. With Map. By Kenneth G. Grubb.

THE MORAL PARALYSIS OF ISLAM. By T. P. Warren.

THE JUNGLE INDIANS OF PERU. By R. B. Clark.

THE PEARL OF THE ANTILLES. With Map. By J. J. Cooksey.

THE REPUBLIC OF PARAGUAY. By Webster E. Browning.

THE EVANGELIZATION OF INDIA. By Alexander McLeish.

Price 3d. each (post paid, 4d.)

LEPROSY IN INDIA: A Survey. 24 pp. With Map. By R. G. Cochrane.
Price 2/- (post paid, 2/2)

LEPROSY IN EUROPE, THE MIDDLE AND NEAR EAST, AND AFRICA. By R. G. Cochrane.
Price 2/- (post paid, 2/2)

LEPROSY IN THE FAR EAST. By R. G. Cochrane. Price 2/- (post paid, 2/2)

A DIRECTORY OF MEDICAL MISSIONS. Compiled by Henry Fowler.
Price 2/6 (post paid, 2/9)

WORLD DOMINION PRESS, 1, Tudor Street, London, E.C. 4

Indigenous Church Series

The INDIGENOUS CHURCH SERIES *deals with the principles which should govern all efforts to plant the Christian Church in the various countries of the world.*

THE INDIGENOUS CHURCH. By S. J. W. Clark. Shoals of letters of appreciation have been received, and their contents could be summarized in the words of one which says: "'The Indigenous Church' should be read by every missionary in the world."
(Second Impression.)   Price 6d. (post paid, 7d.)

With an appreciation of Mr. Clark's work by Roland Allen.

THE FIRST STAGE IN THE CHRISTIAN OCCUPATION OF RURAL CHINA. By S. J. W. Clark.   Pric 3d. (post paid, 4d.)

CHURCH PLANTING. By S. G. Peill and W. F. Rowlands.
                                                           Price 4d. (post paid, 5d.)
INDIGENOUS IDEALS IN PRACTICE. By W. F. Rowlands. (Second Impression.)
                                                           Price 6d. (post paid, 7d.)

THE WAY TO WIN THE WHOLE WORLD FOR CHRIST. By J. MacGowan. A powerful plea for widespread evangelism.
                                                           Price 4d. (post paid, 5d.)

EDUCATION IN THE NATIVE CHURCH. By Roland Allen. Contains a comparison of two opposed conceptions of the Native Church, and a comparison of the divergent conceptions of Christian Education which spring from each. (Second Impression.)   Price 6d. (post paid, 7d.)

THE ESTABLISHMENT OF THE CHURCH IN THE MISSION FIELD: A Critical Dialogue. By Roland Allen. Price 6d. (post paid, 7d.)

THE REAL SIGNIFICANCE OF DEVOLUTION. By Roland Allen and Alexander McLeish.   Price 6d. (post paid, 7d.)

THE CHINESE INDIGENOUS CHURCH MOVEMENT: Some of its Problems. By Violet M. Grubb.   Price 6d. (post paid, 7d.)

INDIGENOUS PRINCIPLES IN NIGERIA. By Herbert J. Cooper.
                                                           Price 4d. (post paid, 5d.)
BASIC PRINCIPLES IN EDUCATIONAL AND MEDICAL MISSION WORK. By Floyd E. Hamilton and Thomas Cochrane.
                                                           Price 6d. (post paid, 7d.)

MISSIONARY METHODS: St. Paul's or Ours? By Roland Allen. The most widely read book on Missionary Principles ever published. A New and Revised Edition. Cloth boards.   Price 3/6 (post paid, 3/10)

THE SPONTANEOUS EXPANSION OF THE CHURCH AND THE CAUSES WHICH HINDER IT. By Roland Allen. Cloth boards.
                                                           Price 3/6 (post paid, 3/10)

"It is a brave book . . . a book which gives one furiously to think; and it is a book which should be well studied by all who realize that not only an extension of missionary zeal but also a reconsideraton of missionary policy is absolutely necessary, if the Church is to face the issues of the World Call with any seriousness."
                                                           —*The Guardian.*

OTHERS WILL FOLLOW

WORLD DOMINION PRESS, 1, Tudor Street, London, E.C. 4